Discovering Kings & Chronicles

THE GUIDEPOSTS BIBLE STUDY PROGRAM

Floyd W. Thatcher   *General Editor*
Robin White Goode   *Associate Editor*
Bob E. Patterson   *Technical Consultant*

The Books of Kings & Chronicles

Discovering Kings & Chronicles   Dr. Arthur F. Sueltz
What This Scripture Means to Me   Barbara Chafin
Cover Artist   Ben Wohlberg
Maps   Jean Norwood

DISCOVERING KINGS & CHRONICLES

The Guideposts Bible Study Program

GUIDEPOSTS ®

Carmel   New York   10512

The photographs on the pages below were reproduced with the permission of the following photographers:
Bruce Cresson: 19 *(top and bottom),* 32, 33, 48 *(top and bottom),* 62, 82, 87 *(top and bottom),* 89, 113, 139, 140, 146, 147
William S. LaSor: 124

Scripture quotation marked (NEB) is from THE NEW ENGLISH BIBLE, © The Delegates of the Oxford University Press and the Syndics of the Cambridge University Press, 1961, 1970. Reprinted by permission.

THE GUIDEPOSTS BIBLE STUDY PROGRAM
Kings & Chronicles
1. DISCOVERING KINGS & CHRONICLES
2. My Working Bible
3. Knowing More About Kings & Chronicles

All Scripture verses referenced herein are from the King James Version of the Bible.

Printed in the United States of America.

Contents

Publisher's Introduction

The Charles Dickens classic *A Tale of Two Cities* opens with these words, "It was the best of times, it was the worst of times, it was the age of wisdom, it was the age of foolishness, it was the epoch of belief, it was the epoch of incredulity, it was the season of Light, it was the season of Darkness, it was the spring of hope, it was the winter of despair . . . "

While Charles Dickens was writing about a later time, his words are most descriptive of that period of Bible history portrayed so vividly in the Books of Kings and Chronicles. Our story is a continuation of the Samuel narrative and picks up with King David's last days and death and the reign of King Solomon (c. 961–922 B.C.)—1 Kings 1–11. Then following Solomon's death we witness the tragic division of the once proud nation of Israel into the Northern Kingdom, made up of the ten northern tribes, and the Southern Kingdom of Judah, composed of Benjamin and Judah. And the story continues until the defeat of Israel and Samaria by the Assyrian armies (c. 721 B.C.)—1 Kings 12:1–2 Kings 18:12.

From that point on, the focus is on the Southern Kingdom of Judah only until Judah is overrun and Jerusalem is destroyed by the Babylonian army under King Nebuchadnezzar in 586 B.C. At that time a large segment of the population including the intelligentsia were forcefully transported into exile in Babylon—2 Kings 18–25.

As we pick our way through this historical epoch we find ourselves amazed at the sophistication of Solomon's "golden years," when Israel's borders were extended to their broadest point and Jerusalem, the City of David, was enlarged to include the magnificent Temple complex. These, along with King David's years, were among the best of times.

Solomon's death and the division of the once proud kingdom ushered in the beginnings of the worst of times. For the most part the rulers of the Northern Kingdom were condemned because of their sin of idolatry and the establishment of the shrines at Bethel and Dan. They were guilty of following the "way of Jeroboam"—of rejecting God and worshiping Baal.

Certain of the rulers of the Southern Kingdom of Judah were viewed more favorably. Hezekiah and Josiah are said to have done "that which was right in the sight of the Lord" (2 Kings 18:3; 22:2). A few other of Judah's kings—Asa, Jehoshaphat, Jehoash, Amaziah, Uzziah, and Jotham—were partially approved of. But the rest of Judah's kings were condemned because they "did that which was evil in the sight of the Lord." These were indeed the worst of times.

To the casual reader, the Books of 1 & 2 Chronicles might seem to be just a rehash of stories that have appeared in earlier books. But in the Septuagint, the Greek translation of what we refer to as the Old Testament books, Chronicles is referred to as "The Things Omitted"—those things omitted from the Books of Samuel and Kings.

But as we discover in our studies, Chronicles was written later and for a different purpose than the earlier books. Following the extensive genealogies that introduce the book, the prevailing theme throughout is worship. The writer of Chronicles wanted his readers to see themselves as a worshiping people—worshiping the one true God who involved Himself in the affairs of His people. In this the Jews were unique among all the ancient people of the Near East.

In a way, the Kings and Chronicles story ends in "the season of Darkness" and "the winter of despair." But as we listen closely to the prophets of those times who spoke for God, we catch unmistakable hints of a coming "season of Light" and "spring of hope." As a part of history, God's story, we know that the God of history is involved in our story.

For the Christian, the "season of Darkness" and the "winter of despair" was driven off the world's scene and ours through Christ's death and resurrection—the "season of Light" and the "spring of hope" the prophets in the world of Kings and Chronicles saw on the distant horizon.

Preface

A research psychologist once put two different pictures into a stereoscope. The left eye saw a bullfighter and the right eye a baseball player. Then he asked several Americans and Mexicans to look into the instrument and tell him what they saw.

The Mexican viewers saw only the bullfighter. The American viewers saw only the baseball player. This simply tells us that apparently what we see isn't dependent entirely on our eyes. And it also suggests that what we see isn't necessarily the sight or the event before us.

When we look out at the world, what we see depends on our history, our assumptions, our hopes, our dreams, our inner vision. You see, we don't necessarily respond to the facts in front of us; we respond to what *we see* the facts to be. Your perception of those facts makes them reality for you. And my perception of those facts makes them reality for me, and that reality shapes my behavior and conditions my mood.

An awareness of this truth helps us understand the Books of 1 & 2 Kings and 1 & 2 Chronicles—that portion of God's Word which occupies our study now. The people who wrote these books looked out at the world and saw the hard facts of life from their perspective. Yet from time to time, in a world that appeared to have lost its nerve because it had lost its way, these writers seem to have caught a heavenly vision. Isaiah, one of the prophets of this period, worded it this way, "In the year that King Uzziah died I saw also the Lord sitting upon a throne, high and lifted up, and his train filled the temple" (Isa. 6:1).

These writers seemed to live with that kind of inner vision. Yes, they looked out and saw the terrible things that were happening in their world. But they also saw the Living God loose in the events of those times. And that inner vision sustained them and gave them hope.

As we study these lessons, we'll notice three things. First, we are studying history, for we have the story in these lessons of what people did. For example, at a time of crisis a man named David appeared on the scene and welded the people of Israel into a nation. That is history.

The Bible is rich in that kind of history. But the Bible isn't all history; the 23rd Psalm isn't history, it is a lyric poem of almost uncomparable beauty. But the story in the Books of Kings and Chronicles is history.

However, we're not only reading history here, we are reading literature. This is more than a bare "congressional record" outlining events and giving facts. The writers reach into the basement of our emotions and demand our attention. Not all writing is literature, for literature affords the reader pleasure that exceeds any description of events. For example, the bare facts in the story of David and Solomon would be rather dry history, but they come to life in living and breathing reality as the biblical writers lay bare the raw edges of the whole story.

But there's something far more important here than history and literature; we have the *Word of God*. God Himself is speaking to us through the people and events. And it is a timeless message.

The Books of 1 & 2 Kings

Originally 1 & 2 Kings was a single book and related to 1 & 2 Samuel. The events in the Books of Kings cover a period of approximately four hundred years. We move from the close of David's reign over Israel and his death, through the reign of King Solomon, the building of the Temple in Jerusalem, and then on to the tragic division into the northern kingdom of Israel and the southern kingdom of Judah. Then the action continues as the writer moves back and forth from south to north and then back to south until the fall of Israel under the Assyrian siege around 721 B.C.

Following the destruction of Israel, the Kings writer continues with the story of the southern kingdom of Judah until it is conquered in 587 B.C. by the Babylonian army.

Throughout the narrative we are supremely conscious that God is the chief Character in the story. The ongoing saga of His grace and mercy and patience is a source of comfort for our times. At the same time this same God is righteous and just in His relationship with His people. Idolatry and rejection brought on the ultimate consequence—defeat, loss of country, and exile by both the people of Israel and of Judah.

Throughout, there is a colorful panorama of kings, some good and some bad. Also throughout there are the prophets of God who remained faithful to God's message. There were Elijah and Elisha. And later came Amos, Hosea, Isaiah. And these were followed by Nahum, Habakkuk, Zephaniah, and Jeremiah. As we study the lives of these spiritual ancestors of ours, we learn valuable lessons for our own pilgrimage of faith.

Seven of our eight lessons in this study follow the events in the Books of Kings. The eighth lesson is a very brief explanation of Chronicles. The Kings scroll or book is thought to have been completed by the time of the fall of Jerusalem and possibly added to somewhat later in Babylon.

The Books of 1 & 2 Chronicles

Chronicles was written many years later after the return of the exiles to Jerusalem from Babylon. The writer of Chronicles covered the same period of history as the Kings writer. But as we will see in our study, his motive for writing and his emphasis were uniquely different.

To cover four hundred years in our Bible story in

13

eight lessons leaves us breathless. But as we participate step by step in the unfolding drama even in this brief study our attention is focused on the God of history. This is His-story, and as the Apostle Paul wrote to his son in the Lord, "All Scripture is given by inspiration of God, and is profitable for doctrine, for reproof, for correction, for instruction in righteousness" (2 Tim. 3:16).

LESSON 1

1 Kings 1–2

The King Is Dead, Long Live the King

Father God, Help me to understand and recognize the truths You have for me in this lesson. AMEN.

A Glorious Background

For many years, David had been a popular leader of the people of Israel. The bands played, the flags flew! He brought grace and style to Judah and then to all of Israel. A warm, vital, clearheaded, energetic man with the heart of a lion and the soul of a poet, David shot across the ancient Near Eastern sky like a flaming star.

In taking a long look at David's life the Chronicles writer had this to say, "Now the acts of David the king, first and last, behold, they are written in the book of Samuel the seer, and in the book of Nathan the prophet, and in the book of Gad the seer, with all his reign and his might, and the times that went over him, and over Israel, and over all the kingdoms of the countries" (1 Chron. 29:29–30).

What times? What times was the writer referring to? I'm sure he had in mind specifically the years David ruled Israel—the period from around 1010 to 970 B.C., forty and one-half years. But we can't help but remember events in his earlier years—events like David, the underdog, taking on Goliath, the Philistine favorite. There's drama in the story of the shepherd boy fighting the massive giant from Gath with only a sling and five smooth stones. The Hebrew writer, with a sense of humor, refers, in comparison, to all the brass Goliath wore and carried (1 Sam. 17:4–6)—brass here, brass there, brass everywhere.

David's times also include his years as a fugitive and outlaw, on the run from King Saul and his forces. Years when he was in exile and forced to live in Philistine territory. And, of course, those years include Saul's tragic defeat by the Philistine army and his suicide on Mount Gilboa, which ushered in David's being crowned king first of Judah and later of all Israel.

The Best of Times and the Worst of Times

With his position secured, David's nobility shines through as he extends grace and kindness to Saul's grandson and Jonathan's son by ensuring that Mephibosheth had an opportunity to live in comfort—this in spite of the fact that Saul had made David's life miserable for so many years. And then we are shown David consolidating and building a nation out of a rather loose confederation of independent tribes.

David's "times" also include the stark tragedy of his sin with Bathsheba and the attempted cover-up through Uriah's murder. While we're not told in just so many words, this whole sordid episode quite likely couldn't help but seriously affect the thinking and attitude of David's sons. After all, he didn't have too good a track record as a father. Apparently, he was no good as a disciplinarian, and then around midlife he models crass adultery and murder.

How much all of this had to do with Absalom's revolt, we don't know. But possibly this episode, coupled with the common people's complaints about the lack of justice and law and order, may well have inspired Absalom's revolt against his father. Let's face it—at least in this time of his life David hadn't set a very noble example.

Dr. G. A. Studdert-Kennedy, a prominent English clergyman and World War I chaplain, commented on one occasion, "The first prayer I want my son to learn to say is not 'God, keep Daddy safe,' but 'God, make Daddy brave and if there are hard things that Daddy must do, give him strength to do them.'

"Daddy dead is still Daddy. But Daddy dishonored is something worse than words can describe."

The whole Absalom episode which ended with his violent death exacted a horrible toll on David who grieved deeply and expressed the wish that he might have died instead of his son. The latter years of David's reign as king were hard years.

An Aging King

Our Scripture lesson opens with rather a pathetic picture. The Kings writer tells us, "Now king David was old and stricken in years; and they covered him with clothes, but he gat no heat [he couldn't keep warm]" (1:1). This once mighty warrior, the giant killer, now about seventy years old, was weak physically and wrapped up in his family's troubles. And yet the times David had lived out were God's times, and God had used them to write on David's soul the pattern of His will and purpose. But now "the music" had stopped. Political intrigue hovered over David's palace like a dark thundercloud; we find him alone and lonely and ill. His physical condition had deteriorated so badly that he lacked body heat.

In the customs of that time, a person in such a condition was given relief by having a young person huddle close so that the body heat would be transferred from the well to the ill. This accounts for the suggestion of obtaining a young virgin who could serve David and lie close to him to keep him warm (1:2).

After an extensive search they located a young and beautiful girl by the name of Abishag who was selected to serve the king. We know virtually nothing more about her except that she was from Shunem, a community in the territory of Issachar, slightly northwest of Jezreel and probably about sixty miles north of Jerusalem. We are told that Abishag "cherished" and "ministered" to the king. It has been suggested that she became a part of David's harem, "but the king knew her not" (1:3–4).

Between Father and Son

David's condition and likely approaching death opened the way for court intrigue. "Then Adonijah the son of Haggith exalted himself, saying, *I will be king*" (1:5, italics mine). Adonijah was David's fourth son, but was now his oldest living son and therefore the natural heir to David's throne. He was now about thirty-five years old and was evidently a spoiled and willful man, because our writer tells us that his father "had not displeased him at any time" (1:6a).

Imagine, David as a father had never corrected his son—"had not displeased him." It sounds as though David was one of the first permissive fathers—a much discussed subject in our time and a weakness so many of us have fallen into. Raising children reminds me of trying to hold a wet bar of soap—too firm a grasp and it squirts right out of your hand; too loose a grasp and it just slides away; only a gentle and firm hold keeps it under control. It is apparent from this description of David's relationship with Adonijah that his grasp had been too loose, and we are about to witness a tragic payoff for parental laxness.

It might be that, because of the rather turbulent life he'd been forced to live, David tended to lean over backwards to avoid being the kind of disciplinarian he should have been. Like so many of us, he may have confused punishment with discipline. But, in reality, discipline has nothing to do with punishment. *Discipline* and *disciple* come from the same root word. And a disciple learns, not from being beaten over the head with rule books, but from emulating someone he or she admires. And because disciples admire a certain person, they voluntarily attach themselves to that one and begin to assimilate their values. In other words, parents who model a life their children can admire and want to follow are authentic disciplinarians. Obviously, as we shall see, David and Adonijah did not have this kind of relationship.

A tragic picture of David's family emerges. First, Absalom stages a revolt against his own father. Now, Adonijah threatens a coup d'etat as his sick and aging father moves through the last days of his life. Apparently neither of these sons saw in the life of their father a model that they wished to emulate. How sad! And yet some three thousand years later the results of a poll taken in 1988 of American teenagers indicate that only thirty-nine percent of them wanted to be like their parents. This simply means that sixty-one percent of these young people did not

Two views of excavations of Old Testament City of David in Jerusalem.

see in their parents a model that they wished to follow. This seems to substantiate the conclusion of the Ecclesiastes writer that "there is no new thing under the sun" (1:9b), while at the same time giving us as parents the challenge of being the kind of people our children want to copy.

Ambitious to Get Ahead

Adonijah's blunt announcement, "I will be king," pictures his ambition in living color as he begins to jockey for position. Allied with Adonijah were his wily old cousin Joab who had been at odds with David several times because of his brutal behavior, and Abiathar, a priest who had every reason to believe that his brother priest Zadok was David's favorite (1:7). Thirst for power had soured all three of the conspirators as they moved to give life and breath to the old phrase, "Power corrupts, and absolute power corrupts absolutely."

Compulsive personal ambition leaves deep and angry scars wherever it is allowed to ride roughshod over our relationships. And this is especially true when the goal is religious power. Power to stack church committees with people who see things *our* way. Power to judge people by *our* standards and exclude those who don't measure up. You've seen those bumper stickers that read, "Love it or leave it"—the idea is love it *my way* or leave.

Then, too, so often in our Western world the so-called religious and the secular seem to get mixed up. On one hand we want to exercise religious power and influence in our real world, and on the other hand we at times try to exclude God from the voting booth or the court room or the school. There are those who want to view the Bible as apolitical—a private witness shrouded in holy neutrality, separate and apart from politics and the nitty-gritty power struggles of life. My use of the terms *political* and *politics* here isn't related to primaries, ward meetings, caucuses, or state and national government. Rather, it has to do with our effort to get along with one another—the art of living together in a complex world and in making the adjustments and concessions necessary to do so.

But the tension between the religious and spiritual

and the "politics" of personal and social concession has always been strong. For example, politics says, "Destroy your enemy," but the Christian faith urges, "Love your enemy." Politics preaches the message that "the first shall be first." But our Christian faith insists that "the last shall be first."

Our task as late twentieth-century Christians, though, is to model a way of life in which there aren't artificial partitions between the secular and religious. God is the God of all of life. In God's world, power plays don't work because He is in charge.

The Other Side of the Coin

We next learn that not all of the key leadership in Israel had deserted David to join forces with Adonijah. Special mention is made of Zadok, Benaiaah, Shimei, and Nathan the prophet—all leaders—as well as the "mighty men which belonged to David." The "mighty men" were an elite group of soldiers who had stood by David over the years. All of these remained faithful to the king and leader who had guided their destinies through the lean as well as the rich times. There was nothing fickle about their loyalties. These were steady men, not opportunists who were interested in feathering their nests at the cost of loyalty to a people and a cause.

A Premature Celebration

So confident was Adonijah of his success that he and his cohorts staged a celebration, a feast. From the description of the location, it seems likely that En-rogel was just below the old City of David in the Kidron valley, not too far from the palace.

But the implication in this scene is more obvious in certain other translations which refer to the sheep, the oxen, and the cattle being "sacrificed" (1:9, RSV). In other words, this blatantly overconfident young man wasn't just guilty of celebrating before the victory was won, he also made this look like a religious celebration in which God was on his side.

There have been "descendants" of Adonijah in every century who have attempted to position God on their side, with their social, political, and economic philosophies. We tend to paint God as a capitalist or a Democrat or a Republican or a Socialist or a member of the Labor party.

21

The Power of a Promise

But as the plot unfolds we see that Adonijah made the fatal mistake of underestimating his opposition and overestimating the weakness of the king, for the next act in the drama features Nathan the prophet in conversation with Queen Bathsheba (1:11–14). You recall it was Nathan who earlier had confronted David over his sinful affair with Bathsheba and the attempted cover-up which cost Uriah his life. Now it is Nathan who gets involved in the intrigue as he tells Bathsheba what is happening and suggests that the queen confront David with his earlier assurance that her son Solomon would be his heir. A promise had been made, but it now looked as though Adonijah would preempt David's intentions.

In response to Nathan's urging, Bathsheba, referred to here not so much as David's wife but as Solomon's mother, runs to the king, who was practically on his deathbed, and said in so many words, "Your son by another woman plans to take over your throne. In fact, right now they're celebrating. Don't you hear the music? And you promised—you promised me you'd make Solomon king after you" (my loose translation of 1:17–21).

David's response to Bathsheba was electric. He may have been practically on his deathbed, but some of the old spark was there, for he responded immediately, "As the Lord liveth, that hath redeemed my soul out of all distress [who has delivered me from all my troubles], even as I sware unto thee by the Lord God of Israel, saying, Assuredly Solomon thy son shall reign after me, and he shall sit upon my throne in my stead" (1:29–30).

David was doing something here that had been characteristic of him throughout all his life—taking an oath, making a vow, and then keeping that vow and promise. David was a man of his word, and he is saying here in effect, "My promise is my promise."

The keeping of a promise, the fulfillment of a vow, is indeed the hallmark of the Christian. When we make and keep promises, we create a small oasis of trust in a desert of unpredictability. When we keep the promises we make, we become more like the God who goes by the name I AM (Exod. 3:14). And it was this same promise-keeping God whose ringing words come to us through the prophet, "Fear thou not: for *I am* with thee: be not dismayed; for *I am* thy God: I will strengthen thee; yea, I will help thee; yea I will uphold thee with the right hand of my righteousness" (Isa. 41:10, italics mine).

A Promise-keeping God

David knew he had a promise-keeping God and that the promises made by His people were sacred and to be kept. And the passing of time has not diminshed that responsibility. The "till death do us part" marriage vows are sacred promises to be kept. The vows we make as parents at the dedication or baptism of our children are to be faithfully kept— not just when we feel like it, but always. We create families and hold them together not because raising children is all fun and games but because of promises made that are meant to be kept.

Human society survives not because people have warm feelings for one another but because of promises kept. It was God's promise that gave birth to a people and a nation that have survived through the centuries to the present. The ancient writer tells us that Abraham heard a voice and started out on an odyssey without really knowing what to believe about either the voice or himself. In spite of all the obstacles Abraham gambled on the reliability of the promises made—and those promises were faithfully fulfilled by Abraham's God (Heb. 11:8–10).

Our late twentieth-century world is extremely precarious and fragile. It seems flooded at times by threat of destruction from our arsenal of nuclear weaponry. And our daily papers carry stories of crime and atrocities that are frightening. But for the people of God—everyday Christians—there is a promise that guarantees the future, for "we, according to his [God's] promise, look for new heavens and a new earth, wherein dwelleth [the home of] righteousness (2 Peter 3:13).

David Acts

Having reaffirmed his promise, David moves to action as he issues instructions to his priest, his army general, and the prophet to take Solomon and crown

23

him king. The orders were crisp and to the point. They were to put Solomon on the king's own mule and go to Gihon, close by Jerusalem in the Kidron valley, and anoint him king (1:32–40). And we're next told that "Zadok the priest took an horn of oil out of the tabernacle, and anointed Solomon. And they blew the trumpet; and all the people said, God save king Solomon." This triggered a great celebration in Gihon. In fact, the writer says the people there were so happy that the "earth rent [was split] with the sound of them [the noise made by the people celebrating]".

Solomon As Co-regent with David

Meanwhile, back at Adonijah's gala, he and all of his guests heard this great commotion and old General Joab picked up the familiar sound of trumpets. And at that moment Jonathan the son of Abiathar the rebel priest came running up with the news that Solomon had been anointed king and was riding David's mule. The fact that Solomon was astride David's mule was significant because in Israel mules were reserved for royalty. It wasn't until sometime later that horses were introduced to Israel's culture (1:41–48). And with that word we witness one of the fastest exits in all the Old Testament, "And all the guests that were with Adonijah were afraid, and rose up, and went every man his own way" (1:49).

With Solomon's hold on the throne of Israel secure, we're next told that Adonijah feared for his life and sought refuge in the sanctuary—"the horns of the altar"—but Solomon assured him that he would be safe as long as he behaved himself (1:50–53).

During this co-regency period while David was still alive, Solomon took careful steps to consolidate his kingdom and establish his authority, and while we don't have a record of it, he undoubtedly was in consultation with his father. And the Kings writer now tells us that when it became obvious that David was dying, the old king gave his son some parting words of advice—"he *charged* Solomon his son" (italics mine). The idea behind this expression is that these words of the dying king were to be regarded as a last will and testament (2:2–4).

In his charge (2:3–9) to the young king David instructed him to do four things: 1) keep the statutes, commandments, judgments, and testimonies of God's laws as they were given to Moses; 2) execute Joab for murdering Absalom, Abner, and Amasa; 3) reward the descendants of Barzillai, the chieftain east of the Jordan who had earlier befriended David; and 4) according to the provisions of the Law (Exod. 22:28), execute Shemei, the man who had put a curse on David (2 Sam. 16:5–7).

David's Death

With the giving of his charge to Solomon in his dying words, David was ready to die. The Kings' writer describes it with great dignity, "So David slept with his fathers, and was buried in the city of David. And the days that David reigned over Israel were forty years: seven years reigned he in Hebron, and thirty and three years reigned he in Jerusalem" (2:10–11).

We learn a little later that David's spears and shields became relics in the sanctuary. And according to the great first-century Jewish historian, Josephus, rich treasures were buried in David's tomb, which was apparently looted on at least two occasions. And so the curtain has fallen on a giant of a man whose greatest accolade came from the Lord through the prophet when He speaks of "David *my servant*" (Jer. 33:21, 22, italics mine).

Solomon—A Man of Authority

With David's death, Solomon's authority over Israel was firmly established (2:12). However, he was soon confronted with a clever bit of palace intrigue instigated by Adonijah, the brother he had forgiven earlier (2:13–25). This time, though, Adonijah made a fatal mistake. Using the queen mother Bathsheba as a go-between, Adonijah asked Solomon to give him the beautiful young Abishag, who had nursed and comforted David through his dying days, as a wife.

While Solomon was the model of respect and courtesy when his mother came to him with Adonijah's request, his response was explosive. He knew well the Near Eastern custom—the one who successfully claimed the king's widow or his harem had the authority to rule the kingdom. He saw through Adonijah's ruse as a challenge to his authority and king-ship and acted immediately to eliminate this half-brother who was determined to undercut him (2:23–25).

Authority is a delegated power. Authority gives the freedom and the right to take action. But authority is dependent on the force behind the user. For example, Prime Minister Gladstone once brought an important paper to Queen Victoria for her signature. The queen didn't like it and refused to sign.

"Your Majesty," said Gladstone, "you must sign this bill."

Victoria turned on her heel and said, "Sir, I am the Queen of England."

Unmoved, Gladstone responded quietly, "Yes, Your Majesty, and I am the people of England." And after a brief period of quiet reflection, Victoria signed the document.

Authority is something that is earned, and Solomon was taking decisive steps in dealing with his challenges.

With the Adonijah matter out of the way, Solomon exerted his authority by eliminating another threat to his power. He deposed Abiathar, the priest who had sided with Adonijah in his rebellion (2:26–27). This left Zadok, the priest who had been faithful to Solomon, in charge.

Next, Solomon moved against another threat to his authority by eliminating Joab (2:28–34), who had defied David's wishes more than once and had joined in the Adonijah revolt. A thirst for power and cancerous jealousy had brought about Joab's downfall from his position as commander-in-chief of David's army and adviser to the king. And his treachery was compounded by the fact that it was the rebellion of a nephew—Joab—against his uncle—David.

Our writer tells us that when Joab heard what had happened to Adonijah and Abiathar, he figured he was next on Solomon's list, so "he fled to the tabernacle of the Lord, and caught hold on the horns of the altar" (2:28b). According to the custom of that time in Israel, Joab would have been safe at the altar in the tabernacle had he been guilty only of rebellion. But he was also guilty of murder. And according to the Law there was no sanctuary at the altar for a murderer (Exod. 21:13–14).

With Joab's execution Solomon's authority is even more firmly established through the elimination of an enemy and the fulfillment of another part of his father's charge. This once great man moved into oblivion as he was "buried in his own house in the wilderness" (1 Kings 2:34)—a reference to the family tomb where his father and brother were buried near Bethlehem (2 Sam. 2:32).

The next action recorded in our Scripture lesson concerns the man mentioned in David's final charge to Solomon, Shimei—a member of the family of Saul (2:36–46). Shimei had placed a curse on David during Absalom's rebellion, but subsequently David had forgiven him (2 Sam. 19:16–23). Apparently, during David's dying days he had come to believe that the curse remained and could only be lifted by Shimei's death. Solomon, however, decided to be merciful. He restricted Shimei to the city of Jerusalem, but warned him of execution if he went anywhere outside the city. We're told that three years later Shimei violated the agreement and the death sentence was carried out.

The final words in our Scripture lesson—"And the kingdom was established in the hand of Solomon" (2:46)—tell us that Solomon's authority was now complete. He was secure as his father's successor to Israel's throne.

Fierce and Uncompromising Times

The raw intrigue and violence involved in David's last days as king and the succession of Solomon to Israel's throne is so foreign to where most of us live that it all seems strange and unreal. At times our Christian sensibilities are probably offended. But we can be reassured by the fact that God used men like David and Solomon to make things happen in line with His eternal purposes.

Solomon, like his father, was very much a man of his times. The struggle to secure the throne that King David had bequeathed to him had been wrenching, and we see him faithfully putting into action his father's charge. Through the struggle to establish his authority as king we get the impression that when he

Jesus' Authority

was at his best he had a sincere desire to live and rule by the laws of God.

All of us struggle daily to establish ourselves in our own worlds in a way that is satisfying and gives us a sense of meaning and purpose. Because of the model Jesus gave us, we know we must take a higher road than disposing of those who seem to be in our way by means of either physical or verbal violence.

As we trace Jesus' footsteps through the Gospels we have a picture of One who serves rather than asserts. Yet, when He spoke people listened. We read that people were astonished at His teaching "for he taught them as one having authority, and not as the scribes" (Matt. 7:29).

And it was this same Jesus who, after His death and resurrection, said candidly, "All power is given unto me in heaven and in earth." Having said that He added, "Go . . . teach . . . and, lo, I am with you alway, even unto the end of the world" (Matt. 28:19–20). Our place is made secure as Christians not by manipulating or playing politics or accumulating power and position as a means of eliminating those who "get in our way," by fair means or foul. Rather, our authority comes from the same Jesus who in His great sermon pronounced a blessing on *the poor in spirit, they that mourn, the meek, the merciful, the pure in heart, the peacemakers, and all who hunger and thirst after righteousness.*

Lord God, I am so glad that my security and position reside in You. Thank You, for Your purposes will prevail. AMEN.

WHAT THIS SCRIPTURE MEANS TO ME
1 Kings 1—2

Reading about King David during his last years reminds me how much life has to do with relationships—parent and child, husband and wife, friends and enemies, self and God. David had been a powerful king. His military exploits and beautiful psalms were well-known. But these last verses about him tell mainly about his relationships with two of his sons and their mothers, with priests and a prophet, and with supporters and old enemies.

I can recall complaining about spending so much time visiting relatives when I was a teenager. But as I have grown older, I find that I increasingly cherish our times together. Family is one of the most basic relationships. I need to nourish that relationship!

And that is not the same as saying that family relationships are always smooth. David's certainly weren't! His wives and children quarreled. One son tried to overthrow him. Two sons tried to outmaneuver each other to obtain the throne. His wife Bathsheba plotted to have Solomon crowned instead of his older half-brother. But however complicated family relationships may be, they still play an important role in our lives.

How satisfying it must have been for David to be able to pass along the reins of leadership to his son Solomon with this sound advice: "Be strong and show yourself a man. Fulfil your duty to the Lord your God; conform to his ways, observe his statutes and his commandments, his judgements and his solemn precepts, as they are written in the law of Moses, so that you may prosper in whatever you do" (1 Kings 2:2–3 NEB).

None of us have given this advice to a son who was king, but many of us have echoed Solomon's words when we have talked to a son or daughter who was about to enter college or university or begin a new job.

David was described as a man after God's own heart (1 Sam 13:14). His relationship with God had always been of prime importance to him. But in looking back over his life, he knew he had not always obeyed God's commandments. He had desired and had taken another man's wife and then had her husband sent into battle to be killed. But when God sent His prophet Nathan to confront him, David had acknowledged his sin and repented.

How good it is to know that God who loves me and expects me to obey Him also forgives me when I repent of my sin and works with me to bring restoration.

Recently I heard Dr. Herbert Reynolds, president of Baylor University, speak to a large group of ministerial students. During the address he told them some of what he had experienced when he had a heart attack several years ago. As the busy chief executive of a large university, he had lived in a world of constant pressures of schedule and agenda. But then he had a heart attack. As he was fighting for his life, he became aware that what was uppermost in his consciousness was not his work at the university but his relationship with God, with his family, and with his friends. The love in those relationships is what sustained him during the hospitalization and long recuperation. And, said Dr. Reynolds, that love is what continues to sustain him each day.

I pray that the love of God, family, and friends will be primary in my life also!

LESSON 2
1 Kings 3–11

Israel's Golden Age—
The Best and the Brightest

Lord God, You are blessed: Teach me Your Word. AMEN.

It was Solomon—the original brightest and best, the man with an outsized personality, a dramatic actor—who brought Israel into a period of strategic power and glory. A modern historian would say that he took advantage of a power vacuum. Babylon and Egypt had both slid into periods of decline, and Assyria had not yet risen to power. So, astride the best trade routes to the Middle East, Israel as a nation was in a position to achieve unprecedented power and prosperity.

Saul, the first king, held court under a tree and later in a fortress, presiding over a loose federation of autonomous tribes. David built a prosperous empire united around a central capital in conquered Jerusalem. Now, under Solomon, Israel's "Golden Age" of power and prosperity had begun.

As we shall see, the Solomon saga began better than it finished. And early on in our story we see a man whose internal conflicts undermined his longing to serve. He seemed to have a modern knack of getting his values mixed up.

Good Advice, Wrong Direction

When William Temple was Archbishop of Canterbury, he told the story about a prankster who got into a hardware store one night and switched all the price tags on the merchandise—lawn mowers were marked two for a nickel, nails were twenty-five dollars apiece, and a gallon of paint was a penny. In commenting Dr. Temple said, "All the values were wrong. That is what has happened to our civilization, and it will not achieve order and peace until our price tags tally with those of God."

Solomon had started out as king with some sound advice from his father—obey God, walk in His ways, and keep the Law—but even in the early stages of our story we begin to see ambivalence. On one hand we see a clever politician who knows what he wants and how to get it irrespective of the cost. On the other hand the Kings writer tells us that "Solomon

Excavated gate of the Old Testament city of Gezer. Gezer was an ancient Canaanite town situated west of Jerusalem toward the coastal plain. It had been under the control of Egypt and had been destroyed. However, it was given to Solomon as a dowry when he married the Egyptian princess. Solomon rebuilt the city.

A high place for pagan worship at ancient Gezer, showing the pillars that are referred to frequently in descriptions of the shrines.

loved the Lord." But he follows that up immediately by saying "he sacrificed and burnt incense in high places" (3:3). In other words Solomon was mixing the use of pagan altars (high places) with worship of the Lord God. We get the idea from the wording here that it was wrong to use these pagan sites for worship of God, and we do know that some of the prophets who came along later denounced this practice as being sinful. Solomon's price tags seemed to shift even at this stage of his life. His heart and his head weren't always together. I know from personal experience that while my head may be only eighteen inches from my heart, they are sometimes the longest eighteen inches in the world.

The opening verse of our Scripture lesson tells us that Solomon made an alliance with the Egyptian

A Marriage of Convenience

Pharaoh and married his daughter as a means of cementing a political relationship (3:1). It is speculated that this Pharaoh was Siamun, one of the last rulers in the twenty-first Egyptian dynasty. World rulers had for years made alliances with foreign rulers by means of marriage, but the people of Israel were forbidden to marry idolaters. (Exod. 34:15–16). Yet after all of David's good advice Solomon marries a pagan princess and brings her right into the City of David.

Then we learn a little later that out of this marriage to the Egyptian princess Solomon received Gezer, a city in the territory of Ephraim that had evidently remained under Egyptian control even though it was located in the central highlands of Israel just a few miles northwest of Jerusalem (9:16).

A Childlike Perspective

In spite of Solomon's early signs of moral and spiritual ambivalence, he got off to a good start. The action shifts to Gibeon, seven miles northwest of Jerusalem, where we're told Solomon went to worship and offer sacrifices to God (3:5–8). It was in Gibeon that the Ark had been kept for a time before David moved it into an especially prepared tent in Jerusalem. We're not told why Solomon went to Gibeon to worship when he could have done it in the Jerusalem shrine, but we are told that God met him there in a dream.

The ancient storyteller describes it this way: "In Gibeon the Lord appeared to Solomon in a dream by night: and God said, Ask what shall I give thee [Tell me, what do you want Me to give you?]." Solomon seems to be overwhelmed as he responds, "I am but a little child" (3:7). In these words we catch a flash of humility as we are reminded of Jesus' words, "Whosoever shall not receive the kingdom of God as a little child, he shall not enter therein" (Mark 10:15). It is the child-spirit in us that is sensitive to the voice of God.

But if the child in each of us is to be open and sensitive to the voice of God, we must have the freedom *to be* and to participate in the adventure of life with joyful abandon and confidence. At the same time, the child within us needs a sense of security, so that we can say, like the pioneer Daniel Boone when someone asked him if he had ever gotten lost, "Never, but there were three days when I didn't know where I was!" Irrespective of outward circumstances, in good or hard times, the Christian is secure in God's love—even if momentarily we don't know just where we are.

An Understanding Heart

Deep in his dream, Solomon responded to the Lord's question, What shall I give you? by saying, "Give therefore thy servant an *understanding heart* to judge thy people, that I may discern between good and bad" (3:9, italics mine). Coming to the throne under the shadow of his father, the great King David, with a vast empire to rule—"a great people that cannot be numbered nor counted for multitude"—and realizing his need, Solomon asked for an understanding, a discerning, a receptive heart. Some translations read a "hearing" or "listening" heart. If Solomon was to know the difference between "good and bad," he needed a heart and mind filled with the wisdom that can come only from listening to the voice of God.

The Ability to Choose

One of the greatest gifts God has given us is the ability to choose, to make decisions. We are not robots that march in step to some heavenly drum. Instead, we choose the kind of life we're going to live. We decide what kind of "heart" and "mind" we will have.

There seems to be a tendency in our fast-moving late twentieth-century world to drift, to "go with the flow." Ours is an "instant world" that doesn't afford us the opportunity for the reflection time so important to making wise choices and good decisions. But to drift, to be influenced by whatever wind of ideas is blowing the hardest, is actually to choose badly and unwisely.

Victor Frankl, the renowned Austrian psychiatrist who survived the rigors of a German concentration camp during World War II noted that prisoners who made it through the horrors of internment were those who chose not to give up. The only freedom the prisoners had left was the freedom to choose their attitudes.

The Art of Listening

Solomon's request for a receptive, listening heart certainly has served as a model for the people of God in all time. But it is important to remember that listening is more than just hearing. Our high-tech world is full of noise which we hear but largely ignore. But to listen to another person brings all of our powers of attention and concentration into focus so that we catch not only what is said but what is meant. Listening for the voice of God—for His guidance—is not something we are likely to do while watching television or playing golf or tennis. Rather, it is something we do in moments of reflective quiet and meditation and prayer.

The Gift of Wisdom

We are next told that it "pleased the Lord that Solomon had asked this thing." In fact, the Lord was so pleased with Solomon's answer that He not only gave him "a wise and understanding heart," He also promised him riches and honor. And then the Lord capped the whole thing off by saying, "And if thou wilt walk in my ways, to keep my statutes and my commandments, as thy father David did walk, then I will lengthen thy days" (3:10–14).

When Solomon asked for the gift of wisdom, he was talking about more than just the possession of information. There's a vast difference between the accumulation of facts and the possession of wisdom. Someone has laughingly said that our colleges and universities are great depositories of wisdom—the freshmen keep bringing so much in and the graduates take so little out!

Our modern society has amazing capabilities for accumulating and storing knowledge. We have electronic brains and computers and calculators with enormous information and storage capabilities. But none of these machines have wisdom—listening and receptive hearts. This comes as a gift from God and from living and believing. Wisdom means understanding in our hearts how to live. We believe in order to understand; we don't understand in order to believe.

You recall the conversation between Jesus and His

disciples. Jesus asked, "Whom do men say that I, the Son of man, am?" The disciples gave the pat answers of the day by telling Him that the people thought he was John the Baptist or one of the prophets. But then Jesus asked, "Whom say ye that I am?" Answering for the disciples, Peter responded, "Thou art the Christ, the Son of the living God." And to this, Jesus said, "Flesh and blood hath not revealed it unto thee, but my Father which is in heaven" (Matt. 16:13–17). This kind of insight and wisdom comes only from God.

A Test for Solomon's Wisdom

Upon awaking from his dream-encounter with the Lord, Solomon returned to Jerusalem, the City of David, and there in the tent sanctuary where the Ark rested he offered his worship and sacrifices to God. Now, he wasn't in any converted pagan "high place" but in the presence of the Lord (3:15). Then follows his first test according to our story (3:16–27).

We don't have any background to the story, but we're simply told that two prostitutes appeared before Solomon and posed a delicate and complicated problem. It seems that each of them had had a baby, but one of the babies had died. Now the claim was made that the mother of the dead baby had pulled a switch in the middle of the night. Each woman said the living baby was hers.

Solomon heard them out and then asked for a sword. When it was brought to him, he said, "Divide the living child in two, and give half to the one, and half to the other" (3:24–25). This judgment flushed out the truth. One woman agreed to the decision, but the other—the mother of the living child—was willing to give up her baby rather than see it killed. And in response, she was given her baby.

The scene closes with a grand affirmation of Solomon by the people of Israel. They respected their king "for they saw that the wisdom of God was in him" (3:28). Solomon was indeed off to a good start. He was faithful to God, and God was with him. This is something we, too, can count on.

A Wise and Capable Administrator

The saga of Solomon's early days as king "over all Israel" now moves from the solving of a personal problem between two women to his administrative ability in ruling a vast nation (4:1–34).

In verses 1–19 we have a list of Solomon's official court family and the twelve district governors he appointed to administer the affairs of the nation. In his wisdom Solomon knew there was just no way he alone could properly handle the affairs of his kingdom, so we see him delegating authority to capable men to act in his behalf.

It is a wise leader of a family, a business, or a nation, who recognizes and accepts personal limitations and delegates responsibility to others. There is just no way that the president of a company, the president of the United States, or the prime minister of Canada or England can personally direct all the affairs for which he or she is responsible. Delegation to capable leadership is the answer. Solomon knew and understood this and the result was a productive and growing nation (4:20–28).

We find in these verses a most colorful description of life during those early days of Solomon's reign: The people of "Judah and Israel dwelt safely, every man under his vine and under his fig tree" (4:25). This description is frequently used throughout the Old Testament to picture a society living in peace and contentment and in prosperity. Solomon, his court, and his appointed managers were doing things right!

Solomon's Fame Spreads

At the close of Chapter 4, verses 29–34, we're given further insight into this remarkable man at this time of his life. "God gave Solomon wisdom and understanding exceeding much, and largeness of heart, even as the sand that is on the sea shore." Here and in the description which follows we see a versatile man—a poet, a writer, a man versed in science—whose fame and abilities were widely known throughout the ancient Near East.

Plans for the Temple

We move now into the beginning stages of the crowning achievement of Solomon's reign, as he makes plans to "build an house unto the name of the Lord my God" (5:5). Hiram, king of Tyre, had been a good friend of David's. So it was only natural that Solomon would turn to Hiram as a source for the

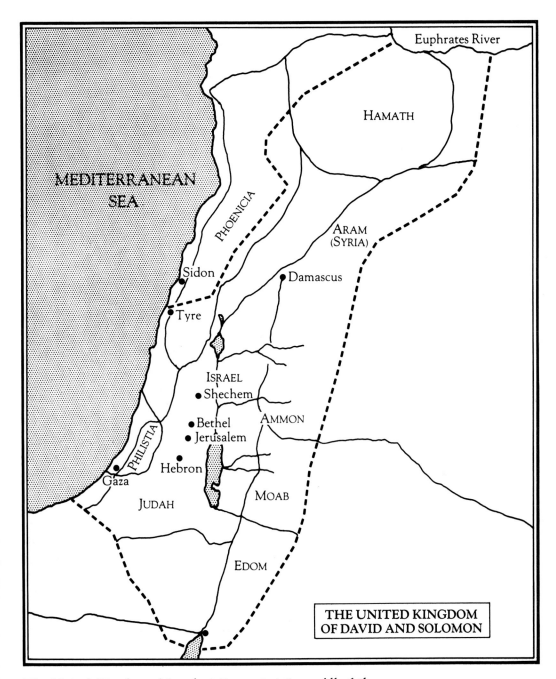

MEDITERRANEAN
SEA

Euphrates River

HAMATH

PHOENICIA

ARAM
(SYRIA)

Sidon

Damascus

Tyre

ISRAEL

Shechem

AMMON

Bethel

Jerusalem

PHILISTIA

Hebron

Gaza

MOAB

JUDAH

EDOM

THE UNITED KINGDOM
OF DAVID AND SOLOMON

The United Kingdom of Israel at its greatest time. All of the area within the broken line to the Mediterranean on the west was administered by Solomon during Israel's Golden Age.

materials that would be needed for the building of the Temple. Their formal diplomatic exchange spelled out the arrangements for obtaining the needed cedar and fir or pine logs for construction and the laborers necessary not only to cut the trees but to float them down the coast so they could be transported inland to Jerusalem. The acquisition of cedar from the Lebanon forests was particularly important to Solomon, as it was considered the finest material available because of its hardwood qualities and its resistance to dry rot (5:1–10).

Solomon in turn would make payment to Hiram in wheat and olive oil. The arrangement was a happy one for both Hiram and Solomon and we're told there was peace between the two countries. The Hebrew word used for peace here is *shalom* and implies a great deal more than the mere absence of hostility. Rather, the idea is that there was a comfortable spirit of wholeness and togetherness prevailing between the two kings and their countries. It was this kind of peace that Paul was referring to when he wrote to the Christians at Philippi, "And the peace of God, which passeth all understanding, shall keep your hearts and minds through Christ Jesus" (Phil. 4:7).

In this spirit of peace Solomon supplied a labor force of Israelites to work with Hiram's laborers in the cutting of trees and the quarrying of the great and costly stones for the Temple (5:17). The Kings writer tells us that the thirty thousand Israelite draftees were on rotation—ten thousand on duty for thirty days in Lebanon and then sixty days at home with their families. Solomon understood the importance, even during this stage, of not having family men away from home over extended stretches of time. We can't help but admire the care and precision that went into all of this planning and preparatory work (5:13–18).

The Exterior Construction

When all the materials had been assembled and transported to Jerusalem, the construction of the Temple began (6:1–10). The first step was the exterior structure which was to be located in an area just outside the walls of the old City of David but within Jerusalem. The Dome of the Rock which can be seen today is on the original Temple site. The main part of the Temple was built in the form of a rectangle thirty feet wide, ninety feet long, and forty-five feet high. It was divided into two rooms: the Holy Place, sixty by thirty, and the Holy of Holies, thirty by thirty. The front faced east, as had the Tabernacle. Huge stones formed the foundation and walls, with the Temple itself being lined with cedar and ornamented with gold.

An entrance hall fifteen feet deep and thirty feet wide was built at the east end of the Temple proper. The entire Temple complex was surrounded by a courtyard. The actual construction began in the fourth year of Solomon's reign.

A Reminder

Following the description of the exterior construction, the Kings writer records that the Lord reminded Solomon again of His promise to be with His people as long as they were obedient in the following of His commandments (6:11–13). He wanted them to clearly understand that the Temple was a symbol of His presence. Their obedience was essential.

The Interior Construction

Next, we are given the details of the interior structure of the Temple (6:14–36)—stone covered with cedar and overlaid with gold. Winged cherubim were fashioned from olive wood and overlaid with gold and were positioned as a guard over the ancient Ark of the Covenant in the Holy of Holies. When completed, seven and one-half years after construction was started, the Temple was a magnificent structure which symbolized God's presence among His people (6:36–38). David's dream was fulfilled at last.

Construction of the Other Buildings in the Temple Complex

With the completion of the Temple proper, Solomon's workmen turned their attention to the construction of the other buildings that were a part of the Temple complex (7:1–12). These included his own palace, the palace for Solomon's Egyptian wife, the House of the Forest of Lebanon (possibly the armory), the Hall of the Throne (the throne room), and the Hall of Pillars (possibly a waiting room for those who wanted to see the king).

Furnishings and Fixtures

With the completion of the buildings, the workmen crafted the furnishings and decorations for the

Temple (7:13–51a). It is virtually impossible for us to picture all that is described in these verses. We can't help but be impressed, however, with the careful attention given to detail. Nothing was left to chance in the construction of the pillars, the altars, the tables, and lamps.

David's Treasures

With the completion of the Temple and all the furnishings, Solomon brought in all the treasures that David had collected and saved over the years (7:51b). These treasures undoubtedly included priceless booty that David had seized from foreign monarchs throughout his reign. All of this had been dedicated to God and rightly belonged in the house of God.

The Dedication—the Ark Moved into the Temple

As we come to the great dedication chapter in our Scripture lesson now, we can begin to sense something of the emotional pitch that swept back and forth across Jerusalem. Construction of the majestic Temple complex just outside the walls of the ancient City of David had taken many years. David's vision of a House for God in Jerusalem was now a reality, and thousands of Israelites had worked and sacrificed in the planning and building of this awesome symbol of their faith in the one, true God—a faith which had unified and bound them together during the centuries leading up to this moment.

With remarkable brevity, the Kings writer tells us that Solomon assembled all of Israel's wise counselors and all of the tribal heads for the dedication ceremonies and celebration. In addition, "all the men of Israel" were present (8:1–2). Then, as a first step, the "elders" brought the Ark of the Lord from its resting place in the old city to the new Temple complex. In addition, we're told "the tabernacle of the congregation"—the wilderness sanctuary—and its furnishings were brought to the Temple complex.

We don't know what was done with the original Tabernacle and furnishings, but we do know that the priests took custody of the Ark and then moved it into the Holy of Holies section of the Temple and placed it underneath the spread wings of the cherubim (8:3–9).

As the Ark rested in its proper place, we're told that "a cloud filled the house of the Lord"—the glory of the Lord God, *Yahweh*, filled the Temple (8:10–11).

As the glory of the Lord filled the Temple, Solomon was deeply moved and offered praise to the Lord in poetic verse (8:12–13), the first line of which does not appear in our King James text. Certain other translations have Solomon opening with a recognition that God had put the sun in the heavens but had said "he would dwell in the thick darkness." While the original intent of this ancient verse may be obscure to us, it is clear that Solomon, as he viewed the Temple now filled with the glory of the Lord, was overcome with praise and adoration.

Following his words of praise, the king spoke to the people gathered in the great Temple complex (8:14–21). In his introductory remarks he reminded them of the events that had led up to the completion of the magnificent Temple as they now saw it. He spoke of how his father, David, had wanted to build the Lord's house but was not permitted to do so. Instead, the task had been assigned to him by David and by the Lord—a task that was now complete because the Ark was in its place and the Lord's glory cloud had filled the Temple.

We come now to the heart of the dedication ceremonies and of this particular chapter—Solomon's prayer of dedication (8:22–53). Solomon faced the altar in the courtyard, and in an attitude of prayer—with hands raised toward heaven—asked God to keep the promises He had made to David (8:23–26); to be ever present in the Temple and receive the prayers offered there (8:27–30); to judge any who might swear falsely against a neighbor (8:31–32); to forgive national sin when it is confessed (8:33–34); to send rain when it is needed (8:35–36); to hear their prayer and help them in times of plague, pestilence, and war (8:37–40); to be receptive to the prayers of strangers or foreigners (8:41–43); to hear their prayer and give them victory in war (8:44–45); to be with them if they are ever defeated and taken into exile (8:46–51); to respond favorably to the prayers of both the king and the people of Israel (8:52–53).

The Dedication—Solomon's Prayer

43

To reflect on this sacred moment of prayer that occurred almost three thousand years ago helps us to discover just how little has changed in our own praying. We too focus on our daily needs and relationships when we pray. And to help us in both our praying and our living, we have Jesus' teaching in His Sermon on the Mount (Matt. 5–7), culminating in the noble yet simple words of the prayer He taught His disciples and which we repeat so often (Matt. 6:9–13).

The Dedication—Solomon Blesses All the People of Israel

In the final act of this dedication drama, Solomon pronounces a blessing on the people, urging them to be faithful in their lives and service so that people everywhere will know about their God. The blessing closes with a call to personal faith, "Let your heart therefore be perfect with [faithful, committed to] the Lord our God, to walk in his statutes, and to keep his commandments, as at this day" (8:61).

With the dedication completed, Solomon and all of the people offered their worship to the Lord through celebrations of prayer and sacrifices (8:62–66). After which they went home happy and joyful "for all the goodness that the Lord had done."

The Importance of the Church in the Life of Faith

In the biblical history the first places of worship were the altars built by the Patriarchs. Then came the portable Tabernacle that served as a worship center for our spiritual ancestors, from Mount Sinai to the building of Solomon's Temple in Jerusalem. And although there have been times of disaster in the Near East and in other parts of the world, temples and churches have served as significant reminders that God still lives in the "presence of His people." The presence of a church building and spire says something to the people in a community. This is true even in the Soviet world where the ancient churches, though many are now no more than museums, give silent witness to the existence of God. It isn't that God is *in* buildings or temples, but now as in c. 957 B.C., when the people of God come together in worship, sacrifice, and fellowship, He is with us, and acts in and through us for the fulfillment of His purposes for us.

In this next part of our Scripture lesson, more than twenty years have passed since David designated Solomon as his successor, and quite a few years since God appeared to Solomon in a dream at the Gibeon worship shrine. In that interval Solomon has solidified the kingdom and completed his buildings at and adjacent to the Temple complex. Now we read that "the Lord appeared to Solomon the second time, as he had appeared to him at Gibeon" (9:1–2).

This time the Lord expresses His approval of the Jerusalem Temple and then gives Solomon the conditions of His ongoing approval (9:3–5). First, Solomon should pattern his life after David's faith. He must live with "integrity of heart"—be sincere and honest in his relationship with God. He was to live out his faith in action and be obedient to God's laws. Finally, he was to honor and live according to all of God's statutes and judgments (9:4).

Then, Solomon is told by God that if he lives in obedience to the conditions just given, he will prosper and his dynasty will go on forever (9:5). In other words God would make good on the earlier promise He had made to David (2 Sam. 7:12–16).

Next follows the warning as to what will happen if the people of Israel do not follow the Lord to obey His commandments and laws (9:6–9). Let's face it, the punishment for disobedience is grim. The Lord will reject them if they disobey His laws and worship false gods. Some picture God in this setting as being harsh, but this is far from the case. The God of the Old Testament is just as much a God of grace as the God of the New Testament. We have the choice and free will to disobey Him and go our own way. But now, as in 900 B.C., we are held accountable for what we do (Rom. 6:23)—but the gift of God is still eternal life, life to the full now and in the future.

Solomon's achievements so far are most impressive. But as we move into this next part of our lesson (9:10–28; 10:14–29), we get an even larger picture of his genius.

Solomon's Second Meeting with the Lord

Solomon's Accomplishments

Shrewd businessman that he was, Solomon built up a prosperous export/import trade (9:26; 2 Chron. 8:17–18). Archaeologists have discovered that Solomon built huge blast furnaces at the port of Eziongeber, turning it into the Pittsburgh of Palestine and in the process becoming the copper king of the Near East. Having no navy, he contracted with Hiram, king of Tyre, to use Phoenician sailors on Israel's ships to create a two-ocean merchant marine that touched port on three continents.

Then, although Solomon's reign was never under severe international threat, he built up an effective army, including a large chariot force and an even larger cavalry. Excavation at Megiddo indicates massive installations for housing horses. In addition Solomon discovered he could make money dealing in military hardware, so he became the greatest middleman of arms in the world at that time. He bought horses and chariots in Egypt and resold them to surrounding nations at a profit.

Our Kings writer tells us that Solomon made silver as common as stones in Jerusalem, and the people of his court had so much gold nobody paid any attention to it (10:21–27). But it was not only a time of prosperity from a material point of view. Israel's golden age was cultural as well. Literature, including the Wisdom writings, flourished, as did science, music, and philosophy. Solomon is credited with producing three thousand proverbs, and one thousand and five songs (4:32–33). In addition, he is credited with lecturing extensively on biology.

We have already carefully studied his building accomplishments. But we discover here (10:18–21) that his throne room was lavish beyond anything we can imagine, and his stock of gold and silver vessels staggers our minds. The oriental splendor described here seems beyond comparison.

The Queen of Sheba

Sandwiched in this section on Solomon's great wealth and possessions is the fascinating story of the visit to Jerusalem of the queen of Sheba, a kingdom in the southern part of Arabia (10:1–13). A man by the name of Sheba is mentioned as the grandson of Abraham by his wife Keturah (Gen. 25:3). It is not unlikely that the inhabitants of the Sheba of Solomon's day were descendants of Abraham's grandson.

Apparently, the news of Solomon's wealth and accomplishments had reached Sheba, and according to our storyteller the queen of that country traveled some fifteen hundred miles to see all of this for herself. Her camels were loaded down with gifts for Solomon when she arrived in Jerusalem, and they were loaded down with gifts from him when she left. As a matter of fact, our writer says that "Solomon gave unto the queen of Sheba all her desire" (10:13). There have been those interpreters since ancient times that have seen sexual connotations in that comment, but we have no proof one way or another.

A Sad Ending to a Good Beginning

We don't know all that happened, of course, because the story of Solomon is told from a religious perspective and isn't intended to be a biographical and historical account. But our Scripture lesson now gives us the tragic story of a man gone wrong (11:1–43). Solomon had amassed money and had achieved power and fame, and somewhere along the line his successes apparently began to get to him. In fact, we are given a clue early in our story when he married a pagan Egyptian princess in order to maintain the friendship of the Pharaoh and get the city of Gezer as her dowry. At any rate, as we reflect on Solomon's wealth, we are reminded of the words of Jesus when He said, "It is easier for a camel to go through the eye of a needle, than for a rich man to enter into the kingdom of God" (Matt. 19:24).

Our writer is very blunt as he moves into this part of his story, "King Solomon loved many strange women." Over the years Solomon had married princesses from virtually all of the nations adjoining Israel. As a matter of fact, our writer insists that he had seven hundred wives and three hundred concubines.

While polygamy was apparently allowable even in Israel at that time, it most certainly wasn't according to God's best plan. Solomon was not merely a polygamist; a large number of the women he married were pagans—something most definitely in violation of God's laws, as we have seen. And to compound

Beersheba was one of Solomon's royal cities. Pictured here are royal storehouses, probably where grain, which was collected as a tax, was stored.

Excavations showing houses at the site of Beersheba.

the problem the Kings writer credits those pagan wives with turning "away his heart" from the truth (11:3).

Next we read that Solomon had turned away from worship of the Lord and "went after Ashtoreth the goddess of the Zidonians, and after Milcom the abomination of the Ammonites." Then comes the blunt label as the writer says, "Solomon did evil in the sight of the Lord" (11:5–6). The description of this once great and wise king is now that of a foolish man who has deserted the faith of his father.

The contrast is vivid. A Solomon obedient to the words of the Lord built the glorious Jerusalem Temple and offered that magnificent prayer of dedication. Now we read about a Solomon who "built an high place [a hill shrine] for Chemosh, the abomination [the repulsive god] of Moab . . . and for Molech, the abomination [the fire god] of the children of Ammon" (11:7). The beginning of Solomon's end is a sickening tragedy. In this part of our story we have a vivid picture of the wages of compromise.

Threat from Without

Throughout much of Solomon's reign peace prevailed. Israel's golden age was possible because there was no threat from foreign powers. Now, however, because of Solomon's sinful behavior the Lord allows enemies to harass Israel. Mention is first made of Hadad the Edomite. The Edomites were descendants of Esau and were constant enemies of Israel, though for much of Solomon's reign they had been at peace. But now the Edomite leader, hearing, no doubt, about Solomon's decline, chose this time to renew the hostility.

In addition to the Edomite threat in the south, we are told that Rezon organized a guerilla band in the north and eventually captured Damascus. The peace that had characterized Israel's life for so many years was now broken.

Rebellion and Intrigue from Within

Not only was Solomon's kingdom suffering harassment on its northern and southern borders, but now there came a rebellion from within, as a man by the name of Jeroboam moves onto Israel's stage (11:26–40).

The story of Jeroboam's rebellion is sketchy. We do know that he was "a mighty man of valour" and was trusted in Solomon's service (11:28). But he apparently turned against Solomon because of his excesses and organized a revolt.

With virtually no further information, we are then told about his meeting with Ahijah, God's prophet, who informed Jeroboam of God's impending judgment which would divide Israel into two opposing forces—ten northern tribes under his, Jeroboam's, leadership, and two southern tribes for Solomon's heir. Ahijah made it clear that all of this would happen because of Solomon's sin of idolatry, of turning away from God.

When Solomon got word of the Jeroboam revolt, he took immediate action, and the young revolutionary was forced to flee to Egypt where the Pharaoh gave him refuge. There he remained until after Solomon's death.

Solomon's Death

With Solomon's death (11:41–43), the consolidation of a great people into a golden era that had lasted for one hundred and twenty years suddenly fell apart. The once noble and faithful Solomon had taken a downhill turn and had given in to the temptations of money and power. Yes, we remember his good years but recoil from the events of his last years. A summary of the last years of Solomon's reign gives us a sad and sordid picture. He taxed the people of Israel unmercifully in order to pay for his follies. And he compromised his allegiance to Yahweh, the Lord God of Israel, by worshiping the pagan Canaanite gods and goddesses.

We can't help at this point but contrast the spirit of Jesus with that of the aged Solomon. Jesus had every chance "to sit in the driver's seat." Power was always within His reach, but instead of exercising that power we see Him with a towel washing His disciples' feet. Over and over again, we see Him in the "servant" role—using His power to heal and help rather than to save Himself from the cross.

As we reflect on the contrasts and ambiguities of Solomon's story, we find in them an enormous challenge and a solemn warning. Few men in either religious or secular history have possessed greater ability. More than once Solomon was told that if he obeyed the Lord and lived a life of holy service, God would use him in a mighty way. At the same time he was warned that it would be disastrous if he turned his back on God. As I look at Solomon's last years, I can't help but echo those familiar words, "There, but for the grace of God, go I." And I find my challenge for the present and the future in the words of the great Apostle who reminds us that "in all these things we are more than conquerors through him [Christ] that loved us" (Rom. 8:37).

Almighty Father, Help me to obey You and live a life of holy, vital service to Your Kingdom. AMEN.

WHAT THIS SCRIPTURE MEANS TO ME
1 Kings 3—11

The chapters in 1 Kings that tell us about Solomon's life are similar to our lives—full of promise and resolve and good deeds, but also full of compromise and sin and failure to obey God.

When I attended Sunday school as a child in Columbus, Georgia, Miss Edwina told stories about Solomon that emphasized his good deeds, especially how he built the Temple in Jerusalem and how he prayed for wisdom. But as I grew older and began to read the larger accounts in the Bible for myself, I became aware of things Solomon had done that displeased God, such as building shrines and worshiping pagan gods with his foreign wives. At first I was distressed that a man who was not good in every way should be included in the Bible. Later I realized that throughout history God has carried out His work through imperfect people who love Him. And then I began to understand that if God could use these people—then perhaps he could also use an imperfect person like me. And it gave me hope!

Like Solomon I have prayed for wisdom. My home has been my "kingdom," and so much wisdom is needed to be a good wife and mother. My husband has said that mothers would make good members of the United Nations because they have so much experience mediating arguments and settling crises. I also need wisdom in setting priorities in the use of my time and energy and talents, both inside and outside my home.

The account of the building of Solomon's Temple has always fascinated me. One of the children's departments in our church built a scale model of the Temple as a learning project and then displayed it in the foyer of the church for all to see. It was a beautiful structure! Through the ages people have wanted to give their best gifts to God. Perhaps that is why so many churches and cathedrals are included on tours. A visit to the Metropolitan Museum of Art in New York or to any of the great museums in capitals around the world reminds us how much poorer we would be without the art treasures that have a religious theme. And then there are the magnificent music, the splendid architecture, and the enduring literature of the centuries! I am grateful that people have dedicated their talents to the worship of God through the ages.

The church I attended as I was growing up had beautiful stained glass windows depicting scenes from the life of Christ. Those pictures were often my "sermon" when I was too young to understand all that the preacher said. I can still close my eyes and "see" those colorful panels—Christ in the manger, Christ calling His disciples, Christ in the Temple at age twelve, Christ as the Good Shepherd, Christ's baptism, Christ on the cross, Christ ascending into heaven. I never knew who the artist was, but his gift enriched my worship then, and still enriches my memory.

It is helpful for me to remember that artists are not the only ones who need to give their best gifts to God. I'm not an artist, but surely there is something I can give. I like the way Christina Rossetti has expressed it in her poem:

> What can I give Him,
>   Poor as I am?
> If I were a shepherd
>   I would bring a lamb;
> If I were a wise man
>   I would do my part;
> Yet what I can I give Him—
>   Give my heart.

LESSON 3
1 Kings 12:1–16:28

History as "His" Story

Almighty Father, As each of my moments slips into history help me to be more and more the person You have called me to be. AMEN.

"Toil and danger are the price of practical wisdom which is bought by the experience of daily life," wrote the Greek historian Diodorus about one hundred years before New Testament times. Then he added, "History is able to instruct without inflicting pain by affording an insight into the failures and successes of others." And from then until now, people have shared the hope that we can learn to understand the present and predict the future by studying the past.

The Hebrews as Historians

The ancient Hebrews, though not gifted particularly as philosophers or scientists, were inspired and dedicated historians. They did a superb job of recording the events of their history.

The stories in our Bible emerge from the earliest of recorded times to roughly A.D. 60. These inspired interpretations make our Bible the inspired Word of God, and in part a record of history.

To learn from history, though, means that we must

find some clear pattern or meaning. As Christian historians, we need to be able to interpret events. And to do so effectively calls for us not to impose any meaning we want on those events. No responsible historian does that.

Interpretations of Historic Events

For example, take the dramatic event which occurred on July 4, 1776, on the eastern seacoast of the United States. An economic historian might report that British mercantile theory had ignited a protest from an exploited market. On the other hand, a political historian might report that the American colonies had declared their independence from England with the ringing of the Liberty Bell in Philadelphia. But years later an inspired Abraham Lincoln put interpretive words to what really happened when he said, "Our forefathers brought forth on this continent a new nation, conceived in liberty . . ."

Both the economic and the political historian would have reported accurately from their particular perspective. But President Lincoln from his vantage point in time saw clearly the deep significance of that first Independence Day. His was an inspired interpretation of the historic event.

History as God's Story

In this way the writer-historians in the Jewish-Christian tradition have attempted to interpret our religious history the way Lincoln did in his Gettysburg Address. We see history as God's story—"His story." For example, an Egyptian reporter writing for the Ramses *Times* sometime around the middle of the 1200s B.C. would likely have reported that a group of slaves managed to escape from a battalion of Pharaoh's army through the accidental help of a strong east wind. But to those Hebrew ex-slaves then and to us now that east wind is seen as a mighty act of God.

History Misread

But unfortunately, because of human weakness and bias we often misread the way God is moving in the events of life. This certainly was a problem for many well-intentioned people during the American Civil War. When the war broke out, ministers in the south predicted victory because they were fighting for what they believed was a righteous cause. They felt that Scripture sanctioned slavery. Therefore, the God of history was on the side of the south.

When the war ended with the defeat of the Confederate armies, many of the same ministers, unable to admit they might have been wrong, saw the results as an act of God's judgment on the sins of the people—card playing, gambling, dancing, and excessive drinking. All of this points to the importance of caution, even as believers, in our interpretations of God's acts in history.

The insightful writers of our Bible understood that God is at the *beginning* of history, at the *middle* of history, and at the *end* of history. God created; He intervened through Jesus Christ; He will make clear His purposes at the end of the story.

Throughout this process humanity is caught up in a massive struggle. But from our perspective we know that Jesus won a decisive battle on Good Friday and on Easter morning. And because of His victory, each little victory since then is a powerful hint of the Ultimate Victory at the future time of God's choosing.

Reading the Signs

How does our little review of the meaning of history apply to what is happening in our Scripture lesson now? Good question!

While many of King David's actions were faithful to the Lord's will, we have seen the moral lapses that occurred throughout his reign. The struggle for power at times involved questionable methods, even in those ancient times. A characteristic of those days all too often was this simple rule, "Do unto others before they do it unto you." A bumper sticker then might well have read, "Help your friends and get rid of your enemies."

When the power shifted to Solomon on David's death, the tactics were very much the same. On one hand we witnessed the merciless elimination of his opposition. On the other hand, his request for a receptive and listening heart brought on a response of blessing from the Lord. Yet as time passed the ambiguities in his actions and life-style pointed toward a godless pattern that moved Israel toward both external and internal threat. The signs of national distress and dis-ease hovered over Israel like an ominous storm cloud.

The End of Consensus

With Solomon's death, his son Rehoboam ascended to the throne in Jerusalem. His rule was apparently readily accepted by the people of Judah in the south of Palestine, but the loyalty of the northern tribes was questionable. So Rehoboam traveled north to Shechem to attend a huge convocation that included all of the northern tribes, because their confirmation of him as king was essential if the kingdom of Israel was to remain intact (12:1).

The selection of Shechem as the location for this meeting was highly significant. Shechem figured prominently in the life of the Patriarchs. Abraham and Jacob had both established centers of worship there. And it was in Shechem that Joseph was buried (Josh. 24:32). It was to Shechem and to Mount Ebal and Mount Gerizim that Joshua brought the people of Israel for the renewal of the Covenant with God after they arrived in Canaan. Yes, Shechem had long been a place of meeting and of decision making for the people of Israel.

Now that the southern tribes of Judah and Benjamin had accepted Rehoboam as their new king, the freedom-loving ten northern tribes gathered to take action, and they came with their own agenda. After all, those ten prosperous northern tribes had paid a heavy toll of blood, sweat, and tears during Solomon's reign as king. They were determined now that things had to change. And they were undoubtedly aware of Rehoboam's wooden and stubborn nature.

It must have been quite a scene in that valley of Shechem between the two historic mountains. A vast sea of tents must have filled the valley as thousands came for this important meeting, which was also attended by Jeroboam who came out of exile in Egypt after hearing about Solomon's death (12:2).

A Simple Request

We have what is probably only a brief digest of the discussions that went on between the elders of the people of Israel and King Rehoboam. "Thy father made our yoke grievous [Your father placed a heavy burden on us]: now therefore make thou the grievous service of thy father, and his heavy yoke which he put upon us, lighter, and we will serve thee" (12:4).

Actually, their request wasn't all that outrageous. They were not asking to get out from under all of the load Solomon's government had laid on them; they were just asking that Rehoboam ease up a bit. My loose translation of this verse reads, "Your father knew how to put in forced labor and he raised taxes on everything to pay for his extravagances. In fact, he got a little out of line. Reduce our taxes and make things easier for us and we'll gladly serve you."

A Call for Time to Consider

Rehoboam's response to the people's request was to ask for a delay of three days before he gave his answer (12:5)—a kind of three-day truce while he tried to think things through. First, we're told, Rehoboam asked advice from the supposedly wise elders who had been faithful to his father Solomon. The idea behind the advice these old counselors gave Rehoboam was to put on an act of being reasonable now and in the end the people would be satisfied and on his side, "If thou wilt be a servant . . . and speak good words to them, then they will be thy servants forever" (12:7).

This advice from Solomon's counselors was more than a little crafty. It says something about the kind of bad advice they had evidently given Solomon during his later years. Usually, we like to think that if we ask advice from older and more experienced people, what we get will be sound counsel. And for the most part that is probably true, but in this case it didn't work that way.

Before making his decision Rehoboam turned to another group of counselors—young men his own age. They urged Rehoboam to take a hard line—show them who's boss! In effect they told him to say, "If you think my father laid a heavy load on you, you haven't seen anything yet. He may have 'chastened you with whips, but I will chasten you with scorpions [leaded scourges]'" (12:10–11). These brash young courtiers who had grown up in the lap of luxury urged the king to straighten out those north-ern rebels by letting them know they were dealing with a no-nonsense man.

The Split Comes

We have no record in this story that Rehoboam asked the Lord for advice during his three days of deliberation. It is true that "there is safety in a multitude of counselors" (see Prov. 24:6), but it is also true that our greatest safety comes from going to the Lord in prayer and asking for His direction. Rehoboam had gotten so far from the faith of his grandfather David that it either didn't occur to him to ask God or he wasn't interested at all in what God might say.

Rehoboam's harsh reply after the three days of deliberation spelled out in blunt language, word-for-word, what his young advisors had told him to say (12:12–15).

When the people of the ten northern tribes heard Rehoboam's response after his three days of deliberation, they announced their declaration of independence, left Shechem and returned to their own homes. The split had come. What had once been a united and powerful kingdom was now divided, and Rehoboam's rule was limited to the southern tribes of Judah and Benjamin, which he governed from Jerusalem (12:16–19).

The Peril of Rigidity

What we do have in this scene, though, is a portrait of a stubborn and willfully inflexible young king. I once watched a willow tree on a very windy day being whipped around so hard I was sure it would break. But it didn't; it only bent under the force and power of the wind. And later, when the wind died down, it stood tall and straight and as perfect as ever.

And then I remembered walking through my town the day after a hurricane had lashed the east coast. Here and there I could see giant trees broken and splintered. These tragic old giants couldn't bend with the force and fury of the wind and were shattered—never again to stand tall as they once had.

Unfortunately, Rehoboam was like these old trees—inflexible, rigid, stubborn, even in his youth. He refused to yield, and in the process his kingdom

59

was broken and shattered, never to be whole again. He flashes across the pages of history as a prime example of a macho, hard-shell, inflexible, uncompromising person. In his egocentric arrogance he refused to see that you don't *rule* people, you *serve* people.

In Rehoboam we have a portrait in living color of what can happen in our church life if we attempt, no matter how righteous the case may seem, to get our way through power plays, conniving, or rigid attitudes. Nor should we bludgeon people into Jesus' great new society we call the church, the fellowship of believers. Rather, they are to be "loved" in. People are attracted to the Christian way of life not through harshness and inflexibility but through an attitude which reaches out to draw everyone in.

At the same time, of course, we understand that the opposite of rigidity is not license. Yes, there are spiritual and moral rules the Christian is to live by. We must not lower Christ's standards. Disobedience to the will of the Lord is sin, no matter how it is clothed. But a rigid, authoritarian hardliner is out of step with the heart needs of people who are hurting and in search of a way of life that has integrity and purpose.

The sacred writer gives his readers of all time the plain, unvarnished truth—the payoff for Solomon's and Rehoboam's mad passion for power has come. "So Israel rebelled against the house of David unto this day" (12:19). In response to the rebellion Rehoboam musters his troops (12:21–24) and plans to crush the uprising. But then comes an order from the highest Authority: "Ye shall not go up, nor fight against your brethren the children of Israel: return every man to his house; *for this thing is from me*" (12:24, italics mine).

The "why" for what has happened emerges clearly now as the Lord speaks through Shemaiah the prophet. Rehoboam, like the power brokers of every century, has run into the God who makes history. Now it comes clear. God has acted in judgment against Israel because of their rejection of Him. Yes, God is a God of love, but He is not indulgent.

There's an important point for us to wrestle with here. God's judgment is quite different from ours. He doesn't judge us the way we do one another. Jesus made that point when on one occasion He said, "I came not to judge the world" (John 12:47). But He had a different kind of judgment in mind when on another occasion He said, "For judgment I am come into this world" (John 9:39).

Let me clarify that distinction. When a person comes into a court of law, he knows whether he is innocent or guilty, but the judge has to find out for himself. However, when God judges a person, He knows the truth already; it is the accused who has to learn it. Unlike human judgment, God's judgment helps us to see who and what we really are. And there is nothing vindictive about God's judgment. Rather, it comes in the context of His love for us, and carries with it forgiveness and acceptance—not merely comfort and healing for a disturbed conscience, but new power to face the future.

While Rehoboam refused to be a "servant" to his people, Jesus clearly understood that leadership and service are not contradictory—the one who leads best, serves most. Allegiance is always strongest where love is deepest. Christ rules our hearts because He died for us. And He points us to a God who knows all about us—the details of our history—and uses neither "whips nor scorpions." Believe me, if God treats us like that, then we should in a spirit of love and mercy treat our neighbors the same way. He is our model, not Rehoboam!

God's Judgment and Ours

We met Jeroboam in our last lesson when he staged a revolt against King Solomon and then had to go into exile in Egypt. But with Solomon's death he returned and is popularly crowned king of the northern tribes (12:20). As the original poor boy who made good, he became a popular leader behind whom all of north Israel rallied.

In Hebrew the name Jeroboam means "May he plead the people's cause"—he was a man of the peo-

A Man of the People

ple who seemed destined to end up in the Hall of Fame for Old Testament kings. You will remember, as we read earlier (11:29–39), that Jeroboam had received the assurance through Ahijah, the prophet of Shiloh, that he would become king over the ten tribes of Israel. With this promise the Lord had also told him, "And it shall be, if thou wilt hearken unto all that I command thee, and wilt walk in my ways, and do that [what] is right in my sight, to keep my statutes and my commandments . . . that I will be with thee . . . and will give Israel unto thee" (11:38).

With that kind of promise from the Lord and the high regard of the people, Jeroboam, we would think, could take charge boldly and set out to become a godly and righteous king. After all, there was no way he could lose with backing like that!

A Fear-Filled Beginning

Instead of boldness, however, we immediately sense feelings of fear and insecurity (12:25–27). We're told that he rebuilt and fortified Shechem in

Excavations at Dan. The steps and platform are probably associated with the shrine and the altar of the golden bull-calves erected by Jeroboam I.

the north central highland and established his capital there right in the middle of a beautiful and fertile valley. He was in control of a vast and rich territory crisscrossed by the popular trade routes of the Near East and with access to the Great Sea.

Our next view of Jeroboam, though, has him speculating "in his heart" about the possibilities of his people turning against him in favor of Rehoboam. Having been a rebel himself, he thought like one and assumed everyone else thought the way he did. Then, too, he began to reflect on the attachment the people of northern Israel felt toward the Temple in Jerusalem. Plainly, as Jeroboam saw it, something had to be done about this.

Then our Kings writer makes an interesting statement, "Whereupon the king took counsel" (12:28). Some commentators interpret this to mean that he took counsel with *himself*—he decided after thinking about it what he should do. If this is the case, not only did he refuse to get counsel from his advisors, but he obviously didn't talk to God about what he should do.

A Convenient Religion

To keep the people of the northern tribes from even thinking about their pilgrimages to the Jerusalem Temple, Jeroboam developed a scheme. He had two bull calves cast out of molten gold and then said to the people, "Behold thy gods, O Israel, which brought thee up out of the land of Egypt" (12:28b). Then he put one of the bull calves in the Lord's shrine in Bethel and the other in the shrine at Dan in the far north. While King David had established the shrine of the Lord in Jerusalem as a unifying symbol to all of Israel, north and south, now Jeroboam sets up rival shrines to separate the people.

It is generally felt that these bull calves were not considered idols but were meant to be visible images depicting God—Yahweh. But even if that were the case, Jeroboam ignored the command of God given on Sinai, "Thou shalt not make unto thee any graven image, or any likeness of any thing that is in the heaven above, or that is in the earth beneath, or that is in the water under the earth: Thou shalt not bow down thyself to them" (Exod. 20:4–5).

In this episode Jeroboam is following the negative example of Aaron who fashioned a bull calf out of gold at the foot of Mount Sinai. Even the call to worship was essentially that of Aaron (Exod. 32:4; 1 Kings 12:28). In both incidents the images would have reminded the people of Israel of the Egyptian and Canaanite fertility gods that surrounded them.

We read also that new priests were selected who were not Levites. The Jerusalem festivals were copied by inventions of Jeroboam (12:31–33). All in all, regardless of the original intentions, the result was a pseudo-religion and, our writer tells us, "this thing became a sin" (12:30a).

Right in the middle of verse 33 we are given rare insight into why all of this went so far wrong. Reference is made to the fact that these had been "devised of [in] his own heart." In other words, these religious ceremonies were his own inventions and their purpose was not religious but political. Jeroboam was using religion to achieve his own ends.

There's sort of a modern twentieth-century sound to this. There are those in our day who use religion for business gain or political acceptance or as a cover socially. We too have our convenience religions that ask nothing of us. And we're sometimes guilty of baptizing our pet ideas and prejudices and practices and then pronouncing them as "the only way to serve and worship God." But as with Jeroboam and his bull calves, his priests, and his festival inventions, our stylized religious patterns and ideas can also become "a sin."

A Bold Word of a Man of God

We know that Jeroboam ruled as king of Israel in the north for twenty-two years (14:20). Beyond what we have already learned, the details of his reign are sketchy. We do know that one way or another his kingdom was in a constant state of hostility with the kingdom of Judah in the south. We know, too, that Jeroboam first established his capital at Shechem. Then he apparently moved to Penuel on the east side of the Jordan River. And finally his later years were spent in Tirzah, approximately seven miles northeast of Shechem. We also know that throughout Jeroboam's reign evil was rampant in Israel. In fact, the

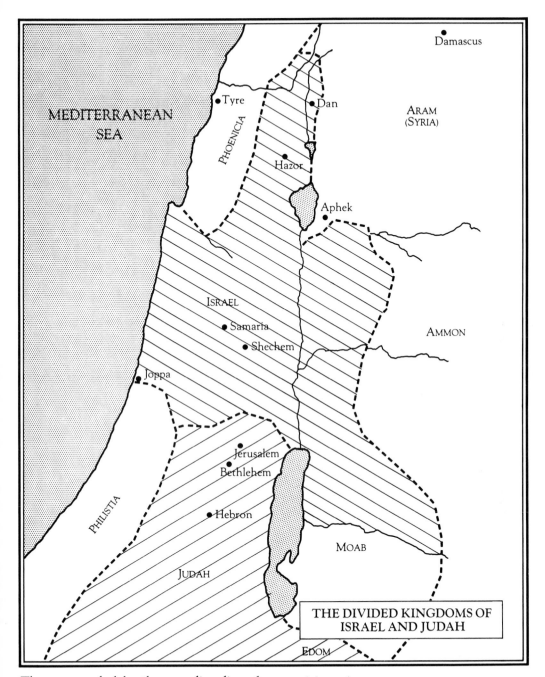

MEDITERRANEAN
SEA

Damascus

Tyre

Dan

ARAM
(SYRIA)

PHOENICIA

Hazor

Aphek

ISRAEL

Samaria

Shechem

AMMON

Joppa

Jerusalem
Bethlehem

PHILISTIA

Hebron

MOAB

JUDAH

THE DIVIDED KINGDOMS OF
ISRAEL AND JUDAH

EDOM

*The area marked by the ascending lines from west to east
(left to right) was the southern kingdom of Judah. The
northern kingdom of Israel is the area marked with
descending lines from west to east.*

Lord's word through the prophet Ahijah states it clearly—Jeroboam has "done evil above all that were before thee" (14:9).

We come now to two revealing and chilling stories. The first is about an unnamed "man of God" who traveled north from Judah and with rare courage publicly denounced Jeroboam and his sins (13:1–34). The unnamed prophet started out by condemning Jeroboam for his evil and idolatrous ways.

Furthermore, the prophet predicted that at some future time a child would be born who was a descendant of David and would become king. This king would destroy the pagan altars Jeroboam had built (13:2)—a prediction that was fulfilled about three hundred years later by King Josiah (2 Kings 23:15–16).

Jeroboam was so outraged at the man of God's public condemnation of him that he raised his arm, pointed to the prophet, and ordered his arrest. The immediate results were electric—the king's arm was either withered or paralyzed and the altar on which Jeroboam had been offering a sacrifice exploded (13:4–5). With understandable panic the king appealed to the prophet to ease God's anger with him and to restore his arm to its former vigor.

While we don't catch any sound of repentance in Jeroboam's words, the prophet prayed and the king was healed (13:6).

The Rest of the Story

The man of God from Judah had been faithful to his calling and to the instructions God had given him, even to refusing Jeroboam's hospitality, but the closing scenes of the story are tragic (13:7–34). Up to this point he had obeyed God's instructions to the letter. But on his way home he was waylaid by a prophet from Bethel who insisted that he too had word from the Lord—a different word than the man of God from Judah had. The messages were conflicting, but our Kings writer says the Bethel prophet lied (13:8).

The man of God from Judah wavered and then went against his own word from the Lord. And from that point on the story takes a strange twist that is difficult for our Western minds to comprehend. But the message is clear and up-to-date. The Christian life is one of obedience to God, not to people. And when we believe we have a word from the Lord—a word that has been tested and tried—we are not to be dissuaded by a word from anyone else. As Christians, we are to test our guidance carefully and then act on it until we have some further word directly from the Lord—not from other people.

We move now into the second Jeroboam story, and it is even more chilling than the previous one (14:1–20). It opens with the word that Abijah, Jeroboam's son, is seriously ill. The king panics at the thought that something might happen to his heir. In his desperation he remembers the prophet at Shiloh who had predicted many years before that he would become king. At the same time Jeroboam is ashamed to approach Ahijah directly, so he sends his wife in disguise. She is to take the aged prophet an offering of food and honey and is to find out what Ahijah has to say about their sick son.

From a Bad Beginning to a Tragic End

Again, there's a twentieth-century sound to Jeroboam at this point. So often, when things seem to be going smoothly some folks forget to go to church, neglect prayer time, and avoid the minister. But when reverses come and trouble strikes, these same folks run to their pastor and ask for his prayers. An authentic faith excites us in the good times and carries us through the hard times!

As we pick up our story again, we discover that the Lord has forewarned the prophet about Jeroboam's attempt to deceive him. And when the queen arrives, the prophet speaks plainly to her. Not only will the boy die but disaster will eventually wipe out Jeroboam and all his heirs. He and all Israel will be judged because they have rejected God and worshiped pagan gods.

Through the prophet Ahijah the Lord pronounced doom on the northern kingdom of Israel "because of the sins of Jeroboam, who did sin and who made Israel to sin" (14:16). We can't help but be reminded here of the words of the Apostle Paul in his letter to the Christians at Rome, "For the wages of sin is death" (Rom. 6:23). The consequences of sin, of rejecting God, are inevitable.

Jeroboam, who as a bright young man had so much going for him, came to a tragic end because he failed to keep God's commandments; beginning with the introduction into Israel's worship of golden bull calves he turned to other gods. And so our writer wraps Jeroboam's life up by saying, "And the rest of the acts of Jeroboam, how he warred, and how he reigned [in war and in peace], behold, they are written in the book of the chronicles of the kings of Israel. And . . . he slept with his fathers [died], and Nadab his son reigned in his stead" (14:19–20). The curtain fell on the ignominious career of a man who paid a high price to forget his God.

Meanwhile Down in Judah

As we have seen in our studies so far, the Kings writer moves back and forth between events in the southern kingdom of Judah and events in the northern kingdom of Israel. Now we look south again for a brief glimpse at the rest of the reign of King Rehoboam. It is easy to get these rather strange but similar sounding names confused. But Rehoboam, you remember, was Solomon's son and heir and through his weakness, stubbornness, and stupidity, he had managed to divide Israel.

In a few words we're told that he reigned as king in Jerusalem for seventeen years. His rule is characterized by these words, "Judah did evil in the sight of the Lord" (14:22). They were guilty of building shrines to the pagan Canaanite gods in "high places . . . on every high hill, and under every green tree" (14:23). In addition, they copied their Canaanite neighbors with the use of male and female prostitutes in their worship.

Within five years from the beginning of Rehoboam's reign, Judah had become a vassal state under the control of Egypt. The Egyptian Pharaoh conquered Jerusalem without a fight and plundered "the treasures of the house of the Lord, and the treasures of the king's house"—the palace (14:25–28). And the curtain fell on the reign of Rehoboam with his death and burial in the "city of David" (14:29–31).

Finally, our Kings writer makes a subtle plant before signing off on Rehoboam, "And his mother's name was Naamah an Ammonitess" (14:31b). It is almost as if he is saying that Rehoboam cast such a blight on Judah and all of Israel because he was the son of a foreign and pagan wife of Solomon. While Solomon's marriages were for diplomatic convenience, in the long run they introduced sinful alliances that led to the corruption of Israel and Judah.

The example here for twentieth-century Christians is clear and simple: Our faith in God and our service for Him must be free from compromise with anything that would diminish or take away from our love and service for Him. True, there isn't danger of our turning to pagan fertility gods like those that were attractive to the people of Israel and Judah at this time. But we have our substitute gods of social position, material worth, political and corporate ambition. Anything, including even marriage and family, that robs God of first place in our lives becomes a sin that can separate us from the Lord and start us down a path away from God.

The North and the South

So for the next fifty years the north and the south fought it out. They fought it out ideologically, spiritually, physically, and economically (Chapters 15–16). About this time the word "Samaritan" came to mean "bad people." To the people in the south in Judah, anybody that came from the north was a Samaritan. They had the same feelings toward the Samaritans that Americans have had for many years toward the Russians. Ideologically, economically, and religiously they just come from different points of the compass. Suspicion and hostility best describe their relations.

Seven Kings in Israel and Judah

Our Scripture for the remainder of this lesson winds down with a chronological description of the reigns of five kings of Israel and two kings of Judah. These strange names and the culture that is so completely foreign to us make the characters seem unreal. But these were very real, flesh-and-blood people who were struggling to establish themselves in their world. Some "did evil in the sight of the Lord," and some did what was "right in the eyes of the Lord."

The first two of the seven kings dominating this part of our lesson are Abijah, son of Rehoboam, and his son Asa. These two ruled the southern kingdom of Judah. The remaining five kings ruled the northern kingdom of Israel—Nadab, the son of Jeroboam; Baasha; Elah; Zimri, who reigned only seven days; and Omri.

Omri, who ruled Israel for twelve years, was the most prominent of this group of northern kings (16:22–28). He is best known in our Scripture account for moving the northern capital from Tirzah to Samaria. Samaria was strategically located on a high hill which was readily accessible to the major routes and highways of that time. The Kings writer tells us that Omri personally bought the land for two silver talents—one hundred fifty pounds of silver or approximately $8,000—and built a magnificent capital city there that remained Israel's capital until the Assyrians defeated Israel in 722 B.C.

Extra-biblical sources give us a little more information about Omri. He is mentioned in inscriptions including the Moabite Stone, discovered in 1868 by an English missionary, as the conquerer of Moab. We also know that he apparently reinstituted friendly relations with the Phoenicians on the Lebanese coast, and it is quite likely this alliance was sealed by the marriage of Omri's son and heir, Ahab, who married a princess from Sidon. Mention of Omri in other inscriptions point to the fact that he was apparently a well-known figure throughout all the ancient Near East.

Asa of Judah

Another king among this group that deserves special mention is Asa of Judah (15:9–23; 2 Chron. 14–16). We're told that Asa reigned as king in Jerusalem for forty-one years. But the most important thing our writer has to say about him is this, "Asa did that which was right in the eyes of the Lord, as did David his father" (15:11).

The Chronicles writer tells us that when Israel under the leadership of young king Asa was threatened by a huge invading army from Ethiopia, he turned to the Lord and prayed, "Lord, it is nothing with thee to help, whether with many, or with them that have no power: help us, O Lord our God; for we rest on thee, and in thy name we go against this multitude. O Lord, thou art our God; let not man prevail against thee" (2 Chron. 14:11). The Lord honored Asa's faith, and Judah's small army defeated the superior Ethiopian forces (2 Chron. 14:12–15).

At such a moment of crisis any practical statesman would have turned to allies for help and support. But Asa refused to allow politics to control his faith in God—a faith unusual in those days. While Asa's record also has its blemishes, he instituted certain reforms that were important to Judah and earned him the Lord's approval.

First, we're told that Asa banished the male and female prostitutes who participated in pagan worship, and he got rid of the idols that previous kings had allowed and worshiped (15:12). Then he deposed his grandmother and destroyed the obscene idol she had erected (15:13). And finally, he placed new treasures in the Lord's house to replace those given to the Egyptian Pharaoh by Rehoboam.

In addition, the Chronicles writer tells us that Asa restored the main altar of sacrifice in the Temple and led the people of Judah in a return to the worship of the Lord (2 Chron. 15:8–14).

The Asa story stands tall in this part of our Scripture as an illustration of the spiritual truth that when we place ourselves on the Lord's side, the odds are unimportant. In his time and culture, he attempted the impossible. In his better moments Asa exemplified the truth Jesus taught centuries later when He said, "With men this is impossible; *but with God all things are possible*" (Matt. 19:26, italics mine).

An illustration in our century of someone who accepted the challenge of the impossible was Anne Sullivan, the instructor who went to Alabama to teach seven-year-old Helen Keller, who couldn't see, hear, or speak. Everyone else had given up, but Anne Sullivan persisted until a breakthrough to the little girl occurred. Throughout our twentieth century Helen Keller has been a magnificent symbol of courage, but it was her teacher and companion who made it all happen, who dared to reach for the impossible.

Our Heavenly Father, yours and mine, wants us to

be people of the impossible. We can, as we pray with Asa, "Help us, O Lord our God; for we rest on thee, and in thy name we go against this multitude."

Merciful Lord, Help me, for I rest in You; I am depending on You, and it is in Your name and for Your sake that I am living. AMEN.

WHAT THIS SCRIPTURE MEANS TO ME
1 Kings 12:1—16:28

Hardly a day goes by that I don't pick up a newspaper accusing a public official of wrongdoing. It's easy to feel that these are indeed the "worst of times." But ours is not the only time that has seemed to be going awry. In our lesson several kings of Israel and Judah are named, and Asa is the only one about whom it could be said that he "did that which was right in the eyes of the Lord" (15:11). Over and over there is the indictment that they "did evil in the sight of the Lord."

In years gone by, unless a public official broke a specific law in our country, there was not much said about integrity. But in recent years, especially since Watergate, there has been an increased emphasis on the importance of character in the realm of politics. During the 1988 presidential primaries, one television commentator explained that since the public had no control over decisions made after a person was elected, the public's only safeguard was to elect a person of integrity.

Does a leader have a higher responsibility than another person? Many people try to make a case for a separate "public" life and "private" life, and argue that they don't affect each other. But it has never worked that way. Leaders are models, whether they like it or not, and the models we choose to follow affect what we do and say and think. "What you do speaks so loudly, I can't hear what you say."

My husband teaches young ministers, and he always asks them on the first day of class to tell him who their model is in the ministry. From that he says he can know fairly well what kind of sermons they will prepare and what philosophy of ministry they have. Leadership models are important—in the nation, in the church, in business, and in the home.

Often we can learn many valuable lessons from those who are more experienced than we are. With the growing number of older adults, there is a wealth of experience available for us today. Rehoboam would have been wise to take the advice of his father's counselors when they suggested that he deal more gently with the people and reduce the conscription labor and high taxes that Solomon had imposed on them. Instead he took the high-handed advice of his own age group and declared that he would be even harder on them than his father had been (12:3–16). As a result the nation was divided into northern and southern kingdoms.

I recall "Brother Joe," our church's resident historian, and the sage advice he gave on so many occasions—advice that was tempered by years of experience. He had a perspective that no one else in the church had. In his later years when he did not hear well, someone asked him why he still came to church when he couldn't even hear the sermon. He replied, "I come because I want people to know whose side I'm on." What a model!

LESSON 4
1 Kings 16:29–22:53

Of Prophets and Kings

Merciful Lord, You are Lord. Help me to trust in You, to not lean to my own understanding; but to acknowledge You in all my ways, knowing with assurance that You will direct my paths. AMEN.

The Books of 1 and 2 Kings might be summarized in this way, "Blessed is the nation whose God is the Lord" (Psa. 33:12) and, "There is a way which seemeth right unto a man, but the end thereof are the ways of death" (Prov. 14:12).

How History Works

From our position in the history and culture of the late twentieth century, we may have some difficulty wading through all these kings who move across the scene in Israel and Judah. In age, they ranged from sixteen up. Some of them ruled as long as fifty years; others moved off the scene in just a short time. Some of them were vicious and some were good.

Collectively, though, their lives illustrate a principle of history that we find in God's story but that also emerges in the writings of such noted historians as Will Durant and Arnold Toynbee. Technically, this principle is referred to as dialectic—every time a bad king appeared on the scene a counter-movement for good emerged. And by contrast, every time a good king moved into history, a counter-movement for evil welled up among the people. That's a generalization, of course, but so far, at least, that has been the broad pattern of history.

Ahab Appears on the Scene

Our lesson opens with the announcement that Omri's son Ahab has now become king of Israel, succeeding his father, and that Ahab reigned as king for twenty-two years. Then the Kings writer tells us what kind of king Ahab was, "And Ahab the son of Omri did evil in the sight of the Lord above all that were before him" (16:29–30), and gives us the reasons for Ahab's reputation.

First, Ahab married a pagan princess who is identified as the daughter of Ethbaal, the king of Sidon. Next, he built a temple and an altar for the pagan god Baal and he began to worship Baal, adding this pagan practice to his worship of the Lord (16:31–33). Finally, one more transgression is listed here (16:34). He rebuilt the city of Jericho—a violation of the word of the Lord at the time of the city's destruction by Joshua and his army. The Lord made it clear then that Jericho was never to be rebuilt (Josh. 6:26). But evidently Ahab felt he needed a fortress city to protect the passageway from the east into Israel's heartland.

An Introduction to Jezebel of Sidon

Since Jezebel figures prominently in our story, let's take a brief look at her background. We learn from secular history that Jezebel's father Ethbaal became the king of Sidon and Tyre by murdering his own brother. His name, Eth-baal, literally means "with Baal." Ethbaal and his family were completely devoted to the Canaanite fertility god Baal who was also believed to control thunder, lightning, and storms. Originally Ethbaal had been a priest in the service of the principal Phoenician goddess Ashtoreth—the Astarte of the Greeks and Romans and Ishtar of the Assyrians. All of this simply means that Queen Jezebel was thoroughly entrenched in the sexual aberrations involved in the worship of the gods of her own people—and, as we shall see, she was a vigorous enemy of the God of Israel.

Elijah Introduced

God's spotlight now illuminates one of the most colorful men in our Old Testament story. Elijah the prophet of God moves onto center stage. Before focusing on Elijah the man, however, it may help to come to a better understanding of just who and what a prophet is. We tend to think of a prophet as someone who foretells the future. While that is true in part, the primary task of the Old Testament prophet was to speak for God—he was called of God to be a proclaimer of God's truth to the people of Israel. He was a messenger of the Lord, led by the Holy Spirit to proclaim the truth.

We have already seen in our story that when a good king is on the throne—doing what is right in the sight of the Lord—the people prosper and all is well. But when a bad king is on the throne, one who does evil in the sight of the Lord, the people are forced to suffer through hard times. And it is during those hard times that prophets explode onto the scene with a message from the Lord. They were those charismatic men of God who followed faithfully in the footsteps of Moses and Joshua.

As the biblical records show, these prophets seem to have an intuitive grasp of real life problems that goes bone deep. Historians interpret events after they happen, but prophets seem to understand the trends of the times while they are happening. We need prophets today just as ancient Israel and Judah needed them, because people continue to worship at the altars of expediency.

Although the two books we are studying are called the Books of Kings, about one-third of the material in them has to do with prophets, who were the real movers and shakers of history. As we shall see, prophets not only experienced the events of their times, they also encountered the meaning behind those events—and again and again that encounter was filled with frustration. To see and feel and then to realize that no one else sees and feels what you do amounts to a kind of dying. Yet they persisted against overwhelming odds to the contrary.

A Modern Prophet

This prophet picture came to mind when I was watching the classic film *Twelve Angry Men.* The action centers around a group of frustrated jurors in a cramped, sweltering jury room. It has been a long trial, and the midsummer New York heat without air conditioning is oppressive. Everybody wants to get out and go home. The prosecutor seems to have come up with an ironclad case proving that the young Puerto Rican had committed the murder. Within just ten minutes after the jury is given the case the foreman calls for a verdict vote.

Around the room, one after another, the word is "guilty" until it is time for one young man to vote. "Not guilty," he says quietly. Everybody is upset and turns angrily on him. Why? In response he shrugs his shoulders in a gesture of embarrassment and admits that he can't point to any evidence—he simply feels in his bones that before deciding on a person's life or death they ought to talk more about the case.

The heat and frustration are stifling. It seems as if nobody is in a mood to reason and be reasonable. Then another vote is called for, and the young man wonders if he shouldn't give in this time and go along with the crowd. But just before they get to him another juror speaks up and says, "The young man is right. We need to discuss the case more."

The mood in the room shifts as they talk on. And when a third vote is called for, another juror joins the first two with a "not guilty" vote. As the discussion continues, the evidence seems to take on a different meaning, and, finally, after what seems like an eternity, a unanimous "not guilty" verdict is announced.

The juror in the film played the part of a prophet. In his bones he had sensed a basic injustice and believed that the majority was following the wrong course. It takes a prophet to stand out in the crowd and speak his deepest feelings, even when it goes against the popular position. This is the kind of prophet we meet in our lesson now.

Elijah and the Drought

With dramatic suddenness Elijah from Gilead, east of the Jordan, bursts into King Ahab's presence in Samaria and proclaims, "As the Lord God of Israel liveth, before whom I stand, there shall not be dew nor rain these years, but according to my word" (17:1). The scene has its comic overtones. King Ahab and Queen Jezebel are relaxing comfortably in their luxurious palace in Samaria—a lush and prosperous part of Canaan. Into this calm atmosphere bursts a crudely dressed and disheveled prophet who announces that no moisture of any kind will fall on the land until he says so. Such unmitigated gall threw Ahab into a fury, forcing Elijah to run for his life to a safe haven by the brook Cherith, near the Jordan river, where the Lord cared for him (17:2–7).

Elijah at Zarephath

In time, the intensity of the drought dried up Elijah's water source. Then God gave His prophet instructions to travel approximately one hundred miles north to the city of Zarephath on the Mediterranean coast about seven miles south of Sidon. There he would make contact with a widow who would look after him (17:8–9). It almost seemed like a fool's errand, but our writer tells us that Elijah obeyed the Lord's instructions. I'm sure the prophet must have wondered why he was making that long trip through a drought-stricken land. But in this scene we have a model of obedience. So often we wonder why certain events occur, but years later as we look back we can see how the Lord led us into life-changing experiences.

When Elijah arrived at Zarephath, he moved into a discouraging situation. The poverty-stricken widow took Elijah in. But when the prophet asked her for something to eat, she poured out her desperation. "As the Lord thy God liveth, I have not a cake, but an handful of meal in a barrel, and a little oil in a cruse." Resigned to her fate, she and her son were going to eat that little bit of food and then give up and die (17:10–12). But the prophet told her to go ahead and use up the food she had to make a loaf and bring it to him. And, wonder of wonders, when she did as she was told she received not only the promise but the reality that she and her son would have all the flour and oil they needed from then on (17:13–16).

A Son Is Restored

Elijah's Zarephath episode winds down with an even greater miracle (17:17–24). The widow's only son becomes ill and dies. In her anguish she blames Elijah. And in these verses we witness a tender scene as the prophet takes the boy to an upper room and there prays for him. Then comes the startling word, "The Lord heard the voice of Elijah; and the soul of the child came into him again, and he revived" (17:22). When Elijah took the boy to his mother, he received the grand affirmation, "Now by this I know that thou art a man of God, and that the word of the Lord in thy mouth is truth" (17:24).

The Reason for the Trip to Zarephath

Now we know why Elijah walked that long, dry one hundred miles from Cherith to Zarephath. While the widow was a native of Sidon, we have every reason to believe that she knew something about Israel's God and she recognized Elijah as a prophet of God. She apparently had some kind of a struggling faith, but after the miracle of the meal and the oil and the healing of her son, her faith grew strong. Israel's God was the God of all people everywhere, even an impoverished widow in the Phoenician city of Zarephath.

But imagine, if you can, what that experience did for Elijah's faith! Twice God had affirmed him by answered prayer. Twice God had acted in response to his pleading. There could be no doubt—God was with him. He could count on God! And while he didn't know it at the time, he was going to need a strong faith in the days to come.

A New Set of Instructions

We get the impression from our lesson that Elijah spent about three years in Zarephath. Throughout all of that time Israel suffered heavily from the drought. But in God's time Elijah got a fresh set of instructions. "Go, shew thyself unto Ahab; and I will send rain upon the earth" (18:1). Once again the prophet was to storm the gates of the king's palace. It was an awesome challenge for a man who had already faced the fury of Israel's king.

Elijah's Return and the Mount Carmel Contest

In obedience to the Lord's instructions Elijah made his way back to the heartland of Israel with the word for Ahab that the time of drought was about over. In the meantime we're told that Ahab and a trusted official by the name of Obadiah (not the prophet) were searching the countryside looking for pastureland for the royal herds. We know nothing more about Obadiah than is mentioned here, but it is apparent that he held a high position in Israel and that he had remained faithful to the Lord in spite of Ahab's and Jezebel's influence.

As the next movement of our story begins to come into focus, we're told that Elijah met Obadiah, whom he undoubtedly knew, and made arrangements for his meeting with King Ahab (18:2–16).

At this dramatic confrontation, Ahab opened the dialogue by saying in effect, "Is it really you, Elijah, you troublemaker?" Our King James translation words it this way, "Art thou he that troubleth Israel?" (18:17). Neither this translation nor my loose one reflect the depth of feeling behind Ahab's question. The implication behind the Hebrew words translated "troubleth" or "troublemaker" is that Ahab believed the prophet was in league with "underworld" or "other-world" sources that had brought calamity on Israel. The depth of the antagonism between the two men is immediately apparent.

Undaunted by the presence of powerful royalty, the prophet refutes the challenge and accuses Ahab of being the real troubler of Israel because he has abandoned the Lord God and has set up shrines to Baal all over the land (18:18). Then follows the challenge that set the stage for one of the most magnificent scenes in the Old Testament—the dramatic contest at a specified location on Mount Carmel between Elijah on the one side, and the four hundred and fifty prophets of Baal and the four hundred prophets of Asherah, on the other. The odds were eight hundred and fifty to one.

The site chosen for this dramatic episode was rich in history. Not far below the Carmel mountains was the scene of Gideon's great victory over the Midianite army. On a clear day the site of King Saul's miserable defeat at Mount Gilboa could be seen, and off to the west was the Great Sea. Now, new history was about to be made.

With all of Israel camped on and around the plateau located about half way up the mountain, Elijah

*The traditional site on Mount Carmel where Elijah
confronted the prophets of Baal is marked by this statue of
Elijah.*

confronted the people and the prophets of Baal and
Asherah with this ringing challenge, "How long halt
ye between two opinions? if the Lord be God, follow
him: but if Baal, then follow him" (18:21). The
prophet was calling for a decision. Either be loyal to
the God of the Exodus, of Mount Sinai, the God who
had been with them in their occupation of the Promised Land. Or be loyal and worship the pagan
Phoenician Baal with its so-called "sacred" prostitu-
tion and child sacrifice. But while Elijah demanded a

decision, "the people answered him not a word."

Now comes the moment of truth. The prophets of Baal are to erect an altar, place an animal sacrifice on it, and then ask Baal to send fire down from heaven to consume the sacrifice (18:22–29). The altar is built, and the sacrifice is laid on it. The prophets of Baal pray and plead, but nothing happens. Then we have a touch of humor as Elijah suggests that Baal may be asleep and possibly, if they call louder, he'll wake up and answer them.

Our writer colorfully describes the desperation of the Baal prophets as the day wore on. "And they cried aloud, and cut themselves after their manner with knives and lancets, till the blood gushed out upon them" (18:28). But by mid-afternoon nothing had happened.

Now the spotlight is on Elijah as he builds his altar, puts his sacrifice on it, and then douses it with water—not just once but three times. The altar, the sacrifice, and the wood were soaked. Then Elijah prayed for the Lord God of Israel, Yahweh, to send fire to consume the sacrifice (18:30–37). Imagine the intense drama of that moment!

The answer came. "Then the fire of the Lord fell, and consumed the burnt sacrifice, and the wood, *and the stones, and the dust, and licked up the water in the trench*" (18:38, italics mine). This was no halfway job. It was proof positive that the Lord was God, the one true God. "And when all the people saw it, they fell on their faces: and they said, The Lord, he is the God; the Lord, he is the God" (18:39). Baal had failed; their Lord was indeed God. Their time of indecision was over, for the present.

Mount Carmel for Today

There have been a lot of changes in the world between the eighth century B.C. when Elijah was at Mount Carmel and the twentieth century A.D., the world in which we live. But it is startling to realize that some of the basic truths that govern human behavior and our relationship with God are very much the same. On Mount Carmel the truth came through loud and clear that we can't be neutral; we can't sit astride a fence. We've got to be on one side or the other.

This was what Jesus was getting at in that part of

His Sermon on the Mount when He said that no one "can serve two masters: for either he will hate the one, and love the other; or else he will hold to the one, and despise the other. Ye cannot serve God and mammon" (Matt. 6:24).

Another significant lesson that comes out of Elijah's Mount Carmel experience is that Elijah didn't play it safe. From the human point of view there was a lot of risk involved when he built the altar, laid his sacrifice on it, and then flooded it with so much water that the water filled the trench surrounding the altar. There was nothing tentative about Elijah's actions; he was "going for broke." His faith in God took him all the way. We can use a strong dose of that kind of faith as we wrestle with the problems of daily life in our world. The Christian is a risker—one with the kind of faith that believes that God is in charge, and His will *will* be done on earth.

The Rains Came

While all of this was going on, we are led to assume that there wasn't a cloud in the sky. Yet the prophet now assures Ahab that rain is on the way (18:41). Then we are treated to a picture of Elijah all alone on the topmost peak of Mount Carmel, looking off to the west with expectancy. At first there is no sign of rain. Yet he maintains his lonely vigil. But after a time Elijah's servant reports that "there ariseth a little cloud out of the sea, like a man's hand." With that, the prophet knows rain is on the way. And soon "the heaven was black with clouds and wind, and there was a great rain" (18:41–46). God had been with Elijah at Zarephath, and He was with him now on Mount Carmel with fire on the altar and a great rain. Elijah saw God acting through all of this. Surely, he would never question again!

Depression and Discouragement

The scene shifts from Mount Carmel east to Jezreel where apparently Ahab maintained a second palace. When the king reported all that had happened on Mount Carmel to Queen Jezebel, she was furious and got a threatening message off to Elijah that she meant to kill him. Jezebel of Sidon was not accustomed to being outsmarted by someone like Elijah (19:1–2).

Jezebel's anger and threat come as no surprise, but what is surprising is Elijah's response. It apparently struck him that everything he thought he had won at Zarephath and on Mount Carmel was about to crumble in fragments around his feet. His world went black. In Elijah I see a man who begins to wonder, "What's the use? Why fight these fierce struggles if, in the end, the evil loose in the world remains as immovable as ever? To fight for justice is one thing. But to fight for justice and have it amount to nothing . . . that is something far more terrible."

Depressed and discouraged, Elijah runs for his life. The price on his head turns his blood to water, and in fear he runs one hundred miles south to Beersheba where he leaves his servant. Then, he continues on south another one hundred and fifty miles to Mount Sinai, deep in the southern desert (19:3–8). Symbolically, it's almost as if he were going back to his roots—back to the place where centuries before Moses had talked with God.

Elijah had gotten food and sleep in the desert, courtesy of an angel, but he still arrived at the mountain discouraged and broken. He felt very much alone and sorry for himself—thinking that the whole world was against him and God had deserted him (19:10). But it is while hiding out in a cave cut into the mountainside that the defeated and discouraged Elijah meets God again (19:9–13a)—not in the earthquake or fire, but in the inward, still small voice.

What a marvelous picture of God's grace and love as He speaks and gives himself to this man who feels so wiped out. God's voice has an awesome sound, quite different from the voice of conscience. It has a shattering grandeur. As Elijah listens, the pieces of his world begin to fall back into place (19:13b–18). He has only one fear left; the fear of God! And this God has a place for Elijah in His plan and there is important work to do. The cure for discouragement and depression was for Elijah first to get physically in shape and then to get busy—anointing Hazael to be king of Syria, anointing Jehu as king of Israel, and anointing Elisha to be a prophet and ultimately his successor (19:19–21).

War . . . War . . . War

Before moving ahead in our Scripture lesson, let's pause a bit and look at the world situation between 885 and 790 B.C. in that part of the ancient Near East we know as the Fertile Crescent—Iran, Iraq, Syria, Lebanon, Jordan, and Palestine. Those were turbulent years. While Egypt in the south had become a second-rate country, the Syrians in the north, while still a fairly small power had begun to test their strength. The ancient trade routes converged on Syria and northern Israel from all four directions. Whoever controlled those routes held the balance of power. We've come to understand this complication better in our late twentieth-century world, as small nations in the Persian Gulf have complicated the lives of the great powers by threatening access to oil rich ports.

North and east of Israel, the Assyrians had begun a general mobilization of their armed forces and were threatening the peace of surrounding nations. Force and not diplomacy determined whether there was peace or war. In short, the ancient Near East in Elijah's time was a powder keg waiting to explode.

Border Wars with Syria

The Syrian threat against Israel was as testy in the ninth century B.C. as it is today. The action in our story shifts now to that northern border. King Benhadad of Syria was harassing Ahab's army and had evidently penetrated as far south as the capital city's fortified walls (20:1–8). Benhadad was pushing Ahab to avoid annihilation by paying a huge tribute of treasure and people. But the hardliners in the Israelite administration urged the king not to give in to the excessive demands that were being made.

Ahab's refusal prompts a crude diplomatic exchange between the two kings, with Benhadad threatening the complete destruction of Samaria (20:9–10). Then as if to outdo Benhadad's insolence Ahab responds by saying, "Let not him that girdeth on his harness boast himself as he that putteth it off" (20:11). While for us the meaning of this is obscure, it has been suggested that it was a familiar proverb of those days that had the same

Pictured here are two panels on the Elijah altar in the
church on Mount Carmel. Portrayed on the lower panel is
the fire consuming Elijah's sacrifice.

force as our proverb "Don't count your chickens before they're hatched."

In spite of Ahab's bravado he is seriously outnumbered, but before anything else happens an unnamed prophet delivers a message from the Lord to the king in which he is urged to launch an attack against the Syrian troops and is assured of victory—*because of the Lord.* Here, as throughout the Bible, God gives surprising victories against staggering odds. The God of Israel keeps breaking into history and arranging great triumphs that turn normal categories and expectations upside down.

In obedience to the prophet's word Ahab launches a massive attack against his superior enemy and wins a smashing victory, just as had been predicted (20:12–21). But in spite of their victory the unnamed prophet urges a continuing defense buildup. They dare not rest easy (20:22).

We get a delightful little twist in verse 23 that gives us insight into the pagan thinking of those times. In the council of war Benhadad held with his advisers after their surprising defeat, they reached the conclusion that Israel won because "their gods are gods of the hills"—Samaria is located in hilly or mountainous country. So in planning their strategy Benhadad and his generals decided on a campaign the following spring that would be fought in the lowlands—Aphek, probably located at a site east of the Sea of Galilee on the highway between Israel and Damascus.

When the Syrian army returned the following spring, they learned that Israel's God was just as present in the lowlands as He had been in the hills, for they suffered a humiliating defeat (20:26–30). Through these two major victories God was trying to show His people that the victories were His—that if they would obey Him, He would be with them. The only way Israel's success could be explained was because God was with them.

The closing scene in this eventful episode sees a peace treaty signed between Syria and Israel, but it is made clear that the conditions are not pleasing to the Lord (20:31–43). In spite of the victories the Lord had given Ahab and his army, they failed to consult with Him in the terms of peace. According to our Kings writer the enemy was to be destroyed, but this was not done.

The Naboth Affair

The setting for the next Ahab fiasco is his summer palace in Jezreel, a beautiful and relaxing spot away from the hubbub of Samaria. From Ahab's point of view everything about the Jezreel palace was perfect except for one problem. Adjacent to the palace was a vineyard owned by a man named Naboth. The king wanted that vineyard but Naboth wouldn't sell (21:1–3). Now, Naboth wasn't just being stubborn in refusing the king; from the standpoint of the ancient inheritance law, he dared not sell it (Num. 27:8–11).

When Queen Jezebel came upon Ahab sulking in bed and not eating, she said in effect, "What's your problem?" (21:4–5). Ahab's answer unleashed all of the cunning Jezebel could muster. She hated the Israelites, their customs, their God, and their values. Earlier, as we saw in the Mount Carmel story she had tried to destroy the people's faith with her hundreds

A scene in Samaria not unlike that which would have been enjoyed by Ahab and Jezebel.

of priests of Baal, the Baal shrines, and the phallic pillars she had erected all over the country.

With a direct attack on Ahab's pride she said in effect to her husband, "Aren't you the king? You run things. You're in charge. But relax. I'll work things out so you get your vineyard" (21:7). Then, taking matters into her own hands she hatched a plot whereby Naboth was falsely charged with a crime that was punishable by death. False witnesses testified to Naboth's guilt and he was stoned—"dead" (21:8–16). And when Jezebel informed her husband that Naboth was dead, he took possession of the coveted vineyard.

The Secular and the Sacred

As we reflect on the Ahab-Jezebel and Naboth story, we may well wonder why it was included by the Kings writer. In response, I would like to suggest that Jezebel represents a thoroughly secular point of view—a pagan religion—and Israel, Ahab's kingdom, represents a people who, even though their belief is faulty and corrupted at times, believe in God who is the Lord of His people. With this kind of a setting in mind, we begin to get a picture of just how the world—the secular—attempts to press its values on Christian believers.

Secular society lets us know in a variety of ways—and one of those ways is television—that Christian morals are outmoded and impractical, that our ideas of sexuality and marriage just aren't workable in today's world. We're made to understand, too, that we should apply the principles of corporate business to our personal and church life—become more efficient and attentive to the "bottom line." At times it may be necessary to bend the rules a bit, but the end justifies the means—after all we live in a real world!

The modern Ahabs and Jezebels may not be as outwardly debased, immoral, and corrupt as their eighth century B.C. counterparts were. They may be smoother and more sophisticated, but the end result of their influence can be just as disastrous. Of course, we Christians need to be able to cope with the complexities of our late twentieth-century world. Our personal and church lives need to be in order. But we're not functioning as a corporate business; we are members of the family of God. And we worship a God who cannot be explained or understood in purely human terms—if He could, He wouldn't be God.

The so-called secular person doesn't and can't understand the Christian Naboths of today. To stand firm and not compromise on values and God's rules for living is completely foreign to the "secular non-believer." This doesn't mean that as people of faith we are to be oddballs in today's world, but we are to hold steady and be sensitive to the fact that God's guidance from our point of view may not always seem practical.

Before returning to our Scripture narrative I want to add one further thought to this part of our discussion. As Christians, we should never draw a line between the "secular" and the so-called "sacred." If there is one thing that our Bible story makes clear, it is that all of life is sacred. All of life—our families, business, vocation, and social life—is realistically meant to be a part of our spiritual growth and development under the guidance of the Holy Spirit.

Elijah Reappears on the Scene

The fiery and colorful prophet once again receives special instructions from the Lord. He is told to confront Ahab with his sin of murdering Naboth and to pronounce the Lord's judgment (21:17–26). The colorful and descriptive words of the prophet are enough to make us shudder as he exposes Ahab's corrupt actions—not only the murder of an innocent man but his licentious and abominable worship of the Canaanite gods. In the prophet's words we hear the awesome voice of God.

Ahab heard, and understood. Elijah's words of condemnation penetrated like a sharp sword. Convicted by Elijah's verbal attack, Ahab repented, if only temporarily, of his sin—he tore his clothes, put on scratchy sackcloth garments of mourning, and fasted. In response to Ahab's repentance the Lord tells Elijah that the judgment against Ahab's dynasty will be delayed (21:27–29). In this we catch another marvelous glimpse of the grace and mercy of God.

Over and over again in the Old Testament as well as the New we are reminded of God's patience and of His mercy. His love is constant, and He longs for a relationship with each of us.

Micaiah of Samaria

Our story line shifts now as we are introduced to Judah's king Jehoshaphat. We first meet him in connection with his visit to Ahab in Samaria (22:1–2). However, we learn more about him toward the end of our Scripture lesson (22:41–53). Here the Kings writer tells us that Jehoshaphat succeeded his father Asa to the throne of Judah when he was thirty-five years old and that he reigned for twenty-five years. The most important thing we know about Jehoshaphat is that "he walked in all the ways of Asa his father; he turned not aside from it, doing that which was right in the eyes of the Lord" (22:43).

On the occasion of Jehoshaphat's visit to Samaria, Ahab proposed that they join forces and attack Ramoth in Gilead, east of the Jordan, a fortress that was still held by Benhadad of Syria. Jehoshaphat agreed but suggested first that they ask the Lord about it (22:3–5). In response Ahab called in four hundred prophets and asked them whether or not Israel and Judah should go into battle at Ramoth-gilead. The response came immediately, "Go up; for the Lord shall deliver it into the hand of the king" (22:6).

Scholars speculate that while these prophets were God-worshipers, they also accepted the idea that it was all right to worship the Canaanite gods as well. They were renegade prophets who specialized in saying whatever they thought the king wanted to hear.

Apparently, their glib reply and demeanor didn't satisfy Jehoshaphat, so he asked if there wasn't a true prophet around they could consult. Reluctantly, Ahab had the prophet Micaiah brought in, but it was under protest because he always came up with bad answers. After a combination of sarcasm and tongue-in-cheek comment Micaiah predicted defeat—he was, indeed, the prophet of bad news (22:7–28).

Ahab's Last Battle

Regardless of the warning, Ahab and Jehoshaphat led their troops into battle. It is described as a long and hard battle, but at its thickest an arrow pierced Ahab's armor, and by the end of the day he was dead (22:29–40). It was the end of an ignominious career.

As the curtain falls on this lesson in our study, we're told that Ahab was succeeded by his son Ahaziah who "did evil in the sight of the Lord, and walked in the way of his father, and . . . mother" (22:52). In order to keep the record straight, the Kings writer tells us that after Jehoshaphat's twenty-five-year reign over Judah he died and was succeeded by his son Jehoram, who had a stormy eight-years' reign (22:50).

We've already mentioned that in the Hebrew Bible what we know as the two books of 1 Kings and 2 Kings was just one book. However, because of its length it was divided into two scrolls. Our narrative continues in our next lesson as we move into 2 Kings.

The End of the First Scroll

While other characters have been on stage throughout this lesson, the predominant one for us has been Elijah, the intensely human prophet. In his life up to this point we've encountered triumph and defeat, boldness and fear. But the trait that has emerged in everything we've seen so far is obedience. In Elijah we have a role model of faith and obedience. We've discovered a sensitive man who learned to listen to the voice of God before he acted—a very hard lesson for most of us to learn.

Savior, Help me to hear and obey Your distinctive voice. Help me to take time to listen for it. AMEN.

WHAT THIS SCRIPTURE MEANS TO ME
1 Kings 16:29—22:53

The last chapters of 1 Kings revolve around three very strong characters—the prophet Elijah, King Ahab, and Queen Jezebel. They were "the movers and shakers" of their period in the history of Israel.

Following years of drought Elijah set up a contest between the Lord and the prophets of Baal on Mount Carmel. While Ahab watched, the prophets of Baal tried unsuccessfully to get their gods to send fire to burn their sacrifice. However, when Elijah prayed, fire came from the Lord and consumed his sacrifice completely.

I once heard a preacher say that we ought to study with the Bible in one hand and a newspaper in the other in order to see the relevance of God's Word for us today. There are so many disastrous situations in the world today—wars, famines, corrupt governments, pollution, illnesses, poverty, and terrorism. I find myself praying that God will raise up another Elijah to lead in overcoming some of today's impossible situations.

I like the challenge Elijah gave the people, "How long halt ye between two opinions? if the Lord be God, follow him: but if Baal, then follow him" (18:21). The course of my life is determined by the choices I make. My choice of friends, of schools, of a mate, of a vocation; decisions about my use of time, talents, and energy. And especially my decision about my relation to Christ.

All through life there are forces pulling me in opposite directions. Sometimes I am made to feel that I must please everyone, and so I become an expert fence-straddler (like Ahab who tried to worship God *and* Baal). What usually happens is that I end up pleasing no one—not even myself. It is impossible to live by convictions, especially Christian convictions, and please everyone.

Deciding to follow Christ can give my life focus. I no longer have to straddle the fence. But after I've made the decision to become a Christian, God doesn't promise that everyone will like me or that I won't have any more problems. Elijah had to run away and hide from Ahab and Jezebel more than once. On one of these occasions he said to God, "I, even I only, am left; and they seek my life, to take it away" (19:10). But God made His presence known and reminded him that there were seven thousand others who were also serving God.

When I feel threatened and alone, it is good to remind myself that God has not abandoned me. One person, plus God, can be a majority. And there is comfort in the companionship of other Christians.

The account of how Jezebel and Ahab schemed to get Naboth's vineyard in 1 Kings 21 is frightening—the ruthless use of power, bribing witnesses, and murder. It reads like a television plot. The late Dr. R. G. Lee, a prominent Baptist minister, preached a sermon on this passage hundreds of times all over the United States. It was entitled "Pay Day Someday." In the sermon he reminded us that God knows about injustice, and that sooner or later He brings retribution.

When life seems unfair and those with ruthless power are running over me, I can remind myself that God loves me and that He will bring a pay day, someday.

LESSON 5
2 Kings 1–12

The Power of Perception

Savior, Help me to hear Your voice even as I study this lesson. AMEN.

What do we know? And how do we know it? The answers to these questions have a lot to do with our powers of perception—our ability to understand and apprehend.

Almost from the beginning of time change has been the one sure thing people could count on. Old landmarks we once thought permanent disappear. Research centers and laboratories pour out torrents of new facts. We're bombarded with information and instant news. Yet, it seems like the more we know, the less we understand.

Most of us become apprehensive in the face of the staggering complexities of a changing world when everything we thought was nailed down starts to come loose. And it all gets terribly personal when you lose a job you had counted on, or a loved one dies, or you're victimized by a prolonged illness. It is then our powers of perception are put to the test, as they were with Elisha, the central human character in this lesson.

But before the searchlight of our lesson focuses on Elisha, we have some unfinished business as we move into the first chapter of 2 Kings, which is just a continuation of where we left off in the last lesson. The Book of 1 Kings closed with the death of Ahab and the coronation of his son Ahaziah as king of Israel.

Now, in this introductory verse to 2 Kings we're told that "Moab rebelled against Israel after the death of Ahab" (1:1). The Moabites were descendants of Moab, Lot's grandson. The land of Moab was situated just east of the Dead Sea, and the people of Moab had traditionally been bitter enemies of Israel until they were defeated by Ehud in the time of the judges. Then Moab remained a vassal state until the defeat of Ahab and Israel's army at Ramoth-gilead. Now, taking advantage of Ahab's defeat, a rebellion is launched by King Mesha.

A description of this rebellion and Israel's response to it is told in detail in Chapter 3 of 2 Kings. A description of Mesha's wars and this revolt is also recorded on the Moabite Stone which was discovered in 1868 by the Rev. F. Klein of the Church Missionary Society in Jerusalem. This heavy black basalt stone shaped like a grave marker contains thirty-four lines in Phoenician writing which describe the wars of King Mesha with Israel.

Unfinished Business

Without doubt, King Ahaziah is a tragic figure. As the son of Ahab and Jezebel, he certainly got off to a bad start, and his two-year reign as king was marked by trouble (1:2–18). In a few cryptic words the Kings writer tells us that "Ahaziah fell down through a lattice in his upper chamber . . . and was sick."

In all probability the palace in Samaria had two or three floors, with the top floor devoted to the king's quarters. It is likely the king's suite opened onto a balcony that had a protective wooden screen. If this was the case, it is possible the king leaned too hard against the screen and fell through it to the ground

A Child of His Parents

below. We do know for sure that he was hurt badly in the fall, and in desperation he sent messengers to the Philistine city of Ekron to find out from the god Baal-zebub whether he was going to live. We have no clue as to why he made his appeal to this particular pagan god, but it is possible this temple was considered a healing shrine.

The name of the Ekron god to whom King Ahaziah appealed for help is quite intriguing. Baal-zebub literally means "lord of the flies," suggesting that he may have been considered a god that prevented plagues which were carried by flies. Irrespective of this speculation, however, it is clear that instead of appealing to God, Yahweh, the king of Israel turned to a pagan deity.

Enter Elijah

While the king's messengers were en route to Ekron, they were intercepted by Elijah. The prophet had gotten instructions to find the travelers and say in effect, "Isn't there a God in Israel? How come you have to go to Baal-zebub in Ekron to find out what you want to know?" Then Elijah concluded his message by saying that the king would die (1:3–4).

The old prophet must have been pretty convincing, because instead of going on to Ekron the messengers turned around and headed back to Samaria. The king asked why they have gotten back so soon and was told about the meeting with the man on the road whose name they didn't even know. The king must have suspected who the unnamed traveler was because when he asked for a description of the man, he recognized immediately that it was Elijah the Tishbite (1:5–8). There's something about the description here that reminds us of a later prophet—John the Baptist (Matt. 3).

Command Performance

Then follows a startling and sobering scene. The king orders the captain of a company of fifty soldiers to find Elijah and bring him under arrest to Samaria. The Kings writer tells us that when the soldiers found the prophet and demanded that he accompany them, "there came down fire from heaven, and consumed him [the captain] and his fifty" (1:9–10).

When word got back to the king as to what had

happened, he sent another company of soldiers after the prophet, and the same thing happened again. In desperation the king sent a third company of armed soldiers after Elijah. Imagine, one hundred and fifty armed soldiers for one unarmed "man of God"! The third captain appealed to Elijah to save their lives by going with them—and Elijah obliged. Back in Samaria and standing boldly before the king, the prophet bluntly declared, "Thou shalt not come down off that bed on which thou art gone up, but shall surely die"—and he did (1:11–18).

Faith Transcends Civil Authority

This story, like so many in the Bible, underscores the importance of faith in God even at the expense of civil authority. When Pope John Paul visited the United States in 1987, he lent his support to the Sanctuary Movement in the United States. The day following the Pope's statement a rather belligerent man cornered me in church and asked, "Where does the Pope get off talking like that? Granting sanctuary for foreign aliens is illegal in this country. Doesn't the Bible teach us to obey the law?" I was caught up short for a moment, and then mumbled, "Which law comes first, the law of God or the law of the land?" Somehow, the Bible keeps raising these troubling questions, and especially through prophets like Elijah.

The Sick and the Dead

This first scene of our story began with a sick king (1:2), and it ends with a dead king (1:17–18). Yet in all of this Ahaziah had a choice in his destiny. It is true, of course, that he couldn't choose his parents or the environment in which he grew up—but he could choose his God. That is why, I believe, that this story comes to us in considerable detail as compared to some of the other "fly-by-night" kings in this lesson. Ahaziah was not a victim. He could have chosen to serve God instead of Baal-zebub. But he decided to live life his way and the consequences were tragic.

Elijah's Grand Exit

Without a doubt, the prophet Elijah was one of the most colorful and impressive men in all of Israel's history. This rugged man of God had a way of dominating any scene in which he appeared, and his fierce

99

denunciations of sin had struck terror into the hearts of royalty and common people alike. In a sense, Elijah is recognized as the father of the prophets. As one of the great figures of the Old Testament, he is known for his vibrant message proclaiming the sovereignty of God and the ethical responsibility of His people. At the same time Elijah is prominent more than once on the pages of the New Testament. Outstanding among those references is the one that places him on the Mount of Transfiguration with Jesus.

Now, our Scripture lesson gives us the privilege of moving along the dusty roads with Elijah and his pupil and successor as they play out the old prophet's last scene (2:1–14).

Traveling from Gilgal near Shiloh—not the one mentioned in Joshua 4:19 which was near Jericho—southwest to Bethel first, and then south and east to Jericho, Elijah with Elisha and a group of young prophets ("the sons of the prophets") are all aware of the significance of this trip. When the two older prophets approach the Jordan, Elijah performs his last miracle as he strikes the water with his mantle, and the two men walk across "on dry ground" (2:8).

On the east side of the Jordan in the general location where Moses was buried, both men know their time together is running out. It is hard to imagine Elijah's deep feelings of emotion as he says to his young friend, "Ask what I shall do for thee, before I be taken away from thee." At the same time we can feel Elisha's sense of awe as he responds, "I pray thee, let a double portion of thy spirit be upon me" (2:9). Acknowledging that only God can grant that request, Elijah suggests that if the young man witnesses his departure the request would be granted.

Then comes the dramatic moment as described by the Kings writer. "And it came to pass, as they still went on, and talked, that, behold, there appeared a chariot of fire, and horses of fire, and parted them both asunder; and Elijah went up by a whirlwind into heaven" (2:11). God had acted!

Carrying Elijah's mantle, Elisha walks back to the Jordan alone. He had *seen* the miraculous exit of his mentor. Now he takes Elijah's mantle and strikes the water. The water parts as it had for Elijah on their way over. Elisha has his sign; he is Elijah's successor with a "double portion" of the old prophet's spirit.

An Alternative World

In all of the Elisha stories I'm anxious for you to catch a glimpse of an alternative world, a world that turns our normal perceptions and expectations upside down. So much of the narrative has to do with perception, the way we see reality. We'll see national leaders becoming minor players and seeming to drift toward the sidelines. The business of kings is shown to be as vulnerable as a house of cards to the real work of this man of God. Because Elisha "saw" the spiritual world, he became a prophet equipped to provide spiritual leadership.

To See or Not to See

Some people "see" and some people do not "see." Blind Helen Keller once asked a friend who had just returned from a long walk in the woods what she had seen. "Nothing in particular," she replied. In reflecting on that Miss Keller said, "I might have been incredulous had I not been accustomed to such responses. Long ago I became convinced that the seeing see little."

All too often our "vision" limits what we think is possible. Recently, I've read about two men who have come up with an interesting "object lesson" that illustrates this point. They describe a scene where a person is grabbed from behind by a strong, rugged man with arms the size of a telephone pole. With his arms pinned to his side the captive leans back and tries to struggle free, but all the wiggling and squirming doesn't work at all.

The captive is convinced it is hopeless. His perception of his captor and his difficulty has convinced him that he can't possibly shake loose and escape. However, Bob Nimensky and Ralph Strauch insist—demonstrate—that with a change of perception the situation can be altered dramatically. By not believing the situation is impossible and by leaning forward instead of leaning back and struggling, the captive changes the center of gravity, and so can jump ahead and shake loose. In other words, by believing the situation is not impossible and by acting in an uncharacteristic manner the results change dramatically.

I realize the problem of generalizing with an illustration like this. However, it points up the truth that our idea of what can be done depends on what we believe to be possible—our perception. This was true of Elisha. The road that brought him to the dramatic moment on the east bank of the Jordan began earlier when Elijah asked Elisha to stop plowing and become a prophet (1 Kings 19:19–21). Elisha was obedient to his call, and his preparation began under the guidance of Elijah. But as important as obedience to a call and preparation is, it wasn't until Elisha saw the chariots of fire and the horses of fire, until he had a vision of God, that he was ready to fill his mentor's sandals and become a miracle-worker himself.

Elisha's experience is meant to be ours. Jesus assured us that "all things are possible to him that believeth" (Mark 9:23)—to the one who has had a vision of God and acts on it. Then a little later Jesus gave to Christians of all time a world-changing promise when He said, "Verily, verily, I say unto you, He that believeth on me, the works that I do shall he do also; *and greater works than these shall he do; because I go unto my father*" (John 14:12, italics mine).

An Affirmation for Elisha

While the "sons of the prophets" from Jericho who were waiting on the west bank of the Jordan had evidently been aware from their vantage point of the whirlwind, they didn't see all that Elisha did. But when they saw Elisha's miracle at the river they realized that the "spirit of Elijah" was with him. But then comes their suggestion that the wind may have just picked Elijah up and dropped him in a canyon somewhere. They propose sending some men out to search the countryside to see if he can be found. While at first Elisha rejected that idea, he finally gave in because of their persistence. As the prophet knew from the beginning, their three-day search was a waste of time. But after it was over, the young men were convinced that Elisha was in fact Elijah's successor (2:15–18).

Now follow in short order two further signs that authenticate Elisha's position (2:19–25). First, the spring that supplied Jericho with water had become polluted. When the people appealed to Elisha for help he asked for a bowl of salt and dumped it into the spring. Immediately the water was purified, "healed"—a further sign of Elisha's role as a prophet of the Lord.

Next, we have a rather puzzling story. Elisha was on his way to Bethel when he was accosted by some "little children" who mocked him and made fun of his bald head. In response our writer says that "he [Elisha] turned back and looked on them, and cursed them in the name of the Lord. And there came forth two she bears out of the wood, and tare forty and two children of them" (2:24).

We probably have only the bare outline of the story. But the same Hebrew word translated "little children" in the King James version can also be translated "youths" or "young men." Then mention is made that the bears mauled forty-two of them. From this we get a clearer picture. Elisha was apparently threatened by a small gang of morally questionable troublemakers. His way of escape was made possible by the intervention of the bears. Along with the healing of the waters, this episode further authenticates Elisha's role as a prophet of God.

From these events so far which give us a bit of a profile of Elisha, we get the impression that he lacks the dramatic and charismatic appeal of his predecessor. Beside the colorful Elijah, Elisha apparently looked and acted quite ordinary. He lacked flair and presence. But in these events at the very beginning of his ministry we see the power of God working through him.

The lesson for us in this interesting comparison is that God uses all kinds of people. He wants to use each of us as we give Him opportunity. There aren't superstars in God's world. Yes, He uses the Elijah types, but He also uses the "quiet people"—the Elisha's of our twentieth century.

Further Confirmation of Elisha's New Role

An Ordinary Prophet

Three Kings and a Prophet

We come now (3:1–27) to the description of the Moab rebellion that was mentioned in the first verse of 2 Kings. Jehoram, Ahab's son, is now king of Israel (c. 852–841). He forms a league with Jehoshaphat, king of Judah, and the unnamed king of Edom. In their plan of attack they plotted a roundabout route to Moab—"they fetched a compass"—that took them through a long dry stretch of wilderness around the southern tip of the Dead Sea, so they could launch their attack from an unexpected direction.

The three kings and their armies ran out of water and the spring they expected to be full was dry. Their situation was desperate. And there's nothing like a desperate situation to cause people to turn to God. That's what Jehoshaphat did when he suggested they needed to consult with a prophet of God. In response to Jehoshaphat's suggestion, one of King Jehoram's officers told the kings that Elisha, Elijah's successor, was in the area. We don't know just how or why Elisha was in Edom, but he was and the three kings looked him up for advice and counsel.

As we read about the meeting of the three kings and Elisha in the southern desert, we can't help but smile at the ironic twist in what is said and done. The haughty prophet seems to step out of character as he makes it clear to Jehoram that he wouldn't be having anything to do with him if it weren't for Jehoshaphat of Judah (3:13–14). But he does tell them that "the valley shall be filled with water" and that the Lord "will deliver the Moabites also into your hand" (3:15–19). Then with a keen eye for description the Kings writer tells us that everything turned out just as Elisha predicted (3:20–27). The kings of Israel, Judah, and Edom—as well as we—are given dramatic evidence that God is in charge and Elisha is his prophet.

Elisha Ministers to Common People in Need

From the moment of Elisha's commissioning by the Jordan River when Elijah left him, the prophet's ministry has been marked by the miraculous. Now in short order we are given several stories that show more of Elisha's quiet miracle-working power. First we have the story of how Elisha went to the aid of a widow by supplying oil for her that could be sold to pay her debts before foreclosure (4:1–7).

Then follows the moving account of Elisha's relationship with the Shunammite woman and her husband (4:8–37). First comes the miraculous birth of a son. And then later when the son is stricken and dies, Elisha, touched by the mother's grief, restores life to the boy.

The scene next shifts back to Gilgal where Elisha miraculously intervenes and offsets the effects of the poisonous stew that had been prepared for the "sons of the prophets" (4:38–41). And next we have the miracle of multiplying the bread so there would be enough for one hundred hungry men (4:42–44). This latter episode reminds us of Jesus multiplying the food to feed the five thousand. In all of this we see Elisha quietly going around meeting the needs of ordinary people.

A "mighty man in valour, but . . . "

In continuing the Elisha saga, we now see him in a different setting. The story begins by describing Naaman, a great man and a general of the Syrian army, but he was a leper (5:1–27). Incidentally, that short description of Naaman is also a picture of contemporary life and society. Like Naaman, our society is great, but with a sickness that threatens our very life. We've inherited freedoms people have struggled for over the centuries. Elaborate machines turn out most of what we need and a lot that we don't need. But we live constantly in fear of the future, are crippled with worry about the state of the world, and feel frustrated and disappointed with our lives. Somehow the meaning of our existence has eluded us. As professor Peter Berger once said, "Here I am, fifty years old and I still don't know what I want to be when I grow up." All of this illustrates a basic human dilemma—Naaman was a great man, *but* . . .

Next, our storyteller speaks of a young Jewish slave girl who was a servant of Naaman's wife. As she went about her daily duties, she could feel the anxiety and depression that hovered over Naaman's house like a dark cloud because of his leprosy. Yes, he still went on the usual glittering round of state functions and parties, but the bleak specter of his illness took all the joy out of it.

Then this little servant girl had an idea. She remembered Elisha and how he had healed people. In so many words, she told her mistress, "I wish my master would go see the prophet who lives in Samaria because he would heal him of his leprosy." When Naaman heard about the servant girl's suggestion, he requested permission to go see the prophet. After all, he had tried everything else, why not this?

Naaman Gets a Poor Reception

With a letter from the king of Syria to the king of Israel and an impressive gift in hand, Naaman was on his way in anticipation of a cure. But when Jehoram read the letter from the Syrian king in which he had instructions to see to it Naaman was healed of his leprosy, he was furious. After all, he didn't have the power or ability to heal leprosy. He was forgetting entirely about Elisha. Instead Jehoram saw this as a plot to put him on the spot (5:6–7).

Word of Jehoram's dilemma reached Elisha, and he sent a message to the king that if he would send Naaman and his entourage to his home, Naaman would then "know that there is a prophet in Israel" (5:8). Obviously, Jehoram was ready for any help he could get. So we now have the delightful scene in which this great general, along with all of his aides and chariots, parked outside Elisha's humble home, waiting for his magnificence to be acknowledged.

But the prophet didn't even bother to come out of the house. He sent a servant out to Naaman with instructions: "Go and wash in Jordan seven times, and thy flesh shall come again to thee, and thou shalt be clean" (5:10). Elisha was suggesting a simple cure, but we read that Naaman drove off in a rage. After all, there were clear and sparkling waters in Syria. Why should he undergo the indignity of washing in the muddy Jordan?

But reason prevailed, and his courtiers encouraged Naaman to do what the prophet had suggested. As a result he was cured, "his flesh came again like unto the flesh of a little child, and he was clean" (5:14).

In the Naaman story we have a foreshadowing of the New Testament Good News—the inner cleansing available through Jesus Christ. Just as Naaman's healing was a gift from God, so the Apostle Paul tells us, "For by grace are ye saved through faith; and that not of yourselves: it is the gift of God" (Eph. 2:8). And for Christians, it is a gift with promise. The writer of John's Gospel tells us that "as many as received him, to them gave he power to become the sons of God" (John 1:12).

Elisha's Miracles Show That God Cares

In the stories of Elisha's miracles we see the longing of ordinary people for a touch of God's power in their lives. We see also that God's grace touches not only kings and prophets but housewives and widows—ordinary, everyday people like we are. In fact, in the next part of our Scripture lesson (6:1–7) we have the story of some men who were cutting down trees with a borrowed axe along the bank of the Jordan River. Much to the consternation of the woodcutter, the head flew off the axe handle and landed out in the river. In response to Elisha's actions the iron axehead floats to the surface and is retrieved—a further sign that Elisha's God is interested in the problems of ordinary people.

With Eyes Wide Open

We come now to an intriguing story in the life of Elisha (6:8–23). The king of Syria, probably Ben-hadad, was waging war against Israel and King Jehoram, but without success. It seemed that no matter what strategy the Syrians set in motion, it was countered by King Jehoram and his army; it was almost as if Jehoram knew in advance what was going to happen.

Ben-hadad suspected there was a traitor in his court, but his advisors assured him that wasn't the case. Instead their problem was Elisha the prophet. He was telling Jehoram what Ben-hadad was going to do—and when. In fact, they believed that Elisha's powers were so great that he was able to tell Jehoram what Ben-hadad said even in his bedroom (6:12–13). With that bit of intelligence, the Syrian king knew they had to get rid of Elisha.

Ben-hadad dispatched a commando force to Dothan, some eleven miles north of Samaria, with instructions to take the city and take care of Elisha

(6:13–14). Imagine! A king sending a small army to apprehend an unarmed prophet of God! This lone prophet from Dothan and Samaria had upset the plans of a powerful king and had wreaked havoc on Syria's foreign policy. Instead of Ben-hadad's being in control, Elisha was.

Now, with the scene set we're ready for action (6:15–19). Dothan is surrounded by chariots, horses, and troops, and that is what Elisha's servant-disciple saw when he looked outside in the morning. In terror the servant turned to Elisha and said, "Alas, my master! how [what] shall we do?" In response the old prophet uttered one of the most magnificent statements in all of the Old Testament, "Fear not: for they that be with us are more than they that be with them" (6:16).

Then Elisha prayed that the Lord would open his servant's eyes. When the servant looked again he saw that the mountains surrounding Dothan were alive with "horses and chariots of fire" (6:17b)—the hosts of heaven were poised to save the man of God.

The servant was now seeing the world from a completely new perspective. With this new unlimited vision everything looked different. It can for us, too. When we look at the world through God's eyes, all things become possible. Real power isn't in the hands of a king or a governor or a president—but with the faithful followers of the Lord.

Seeing and Not Seeing

First, Elisha had asked God to help his servant see. Now he prays again, but this time he asks God to keep the Syrian commando force from seeing. Suddenly the blind see but the seeing go blind. Elisha prayed, "Smite this people I pray thee, with blindness" (6:18). The Hebrew word for "blindness" here can also mean "confused sight," and that is likely what happened.

Then follows a delightful bit of humor. With the sight of the Syrian commando force confused, the prophet next tells them that they're in the wrong place, and he offers to take them where they are supposed to be. And with that he leads them across the countryside to Samaria (6:18–19). Once they are inside the city walls Elisha then prays that the Syrians' eyes will be opened. Only then did they discover where they were.

When the king of Israel wanted to wipe out the enemy, Elisha refused to let that happen. Instead they fed the captive soldiers and then sent them back to Damascus in Syria (6:21–23). An amazing story involving two powerful ancient Near Eastern rulers! But who's in charge of the action? The prophet of the Lord. And there was peace—for a time at least.

Samaria under Siege

The Kings writer next gives us a vivid description of a Syrian attack on Samaria, Israel's capital city. It is important to remember at this point that the writer is telling a series of stories that are not necessarily in chronological order. While history is involved, our primary interest is in seeing God at work through the prophet Elisha. A horror picture emerges as we see a city under siege and a people without food (6:24–33). The situation became so desperate that the people resorted to cannibalism.

The king is outraged and blames Elisha for what is happening. He orders Elisha's execution. But the prophet remained impassive. Yes, his executioner was on the way, but he also seemed to know that the king himself was close behind. So, through a ruse the executioner was delayed, and when the king arrived, Elisha had a special message for him.

Deliverance

When the king arrived, the prophet was ready for him with a message alive with good news and hope for the future (7:1–20). In fact, so important is his message that for the first time he opens with, "Hear ye the word of the Lord; Thus saith the Lord" (7:1). It was important for the king to know without question that what Elisha was about to say was indeed from God. Then he announces that by tomorrow at this time Samaria will be free from the siege of the Syrian army.

As you read this delightful story, I'm sure you'll catch the humor. Picture the scene: The Syrian army has the walled city of Samaria completely boxed in. So far the Israelites are at their mercy. But then in the blackness of night "the Lord had made the host of the Syrians to hear a noise of chariots, and a noise of horses, even the noise of a great host" (7:6). Immediately they surmised that the Egyptians from the south and the Hittites from the north had come to help Israel.

Assuming they were about to be trapped, the Syrian soldiers abandoned their camp, their chariots, their horses, and all of their supplies and headed for Damascus on the run. The God who could open peoples' eyes so they could see, or close them so they were confused and couldn't see, had now created sounds that terrorized an entire army.

In the meantime everything had been quiet in Samaria. The Syrian retreat was discovered only when four desperate and hungry lepers in search of food saw that the Syrian camp was deserted. And it was they who informed the guards on duty at the gate that their enemies were gone. Not only were they gone, but now all of their supplies and animals were in the hands of the hungry Samaritans. Elisha's prediction of the day before had been fulfilled to the letter.

The Damascus Revolt

Very briefly now the Kings writer gives us the rest of the story of the woman of Shunem from where it had left off (4:37) and tells us how she was ultimately rewarded for her care of Elisha (8:1–6). Then he continues on with the account of the kings of Israel and Judah. But first we have a bit of high drama in Damascus and Elisha's involvement with what happened (8:7–15).

This unusual story has Elisha in the Syrian city of Damascus—enemy territory. But because of his reputation as a man of God he was safe. In fact, when King Ben-hadad heard he was in the city, he sent Hazael, his personal emissary, to ask the prophet whether he, the king, would recover from his illness.

While Elisha seemed to reassure Ben-hadad, with prophetic insight he told Hazael that he knew the king would not recover and that in fact Hazael would become king. Feigning humility Hazael decryed the possibility, but it is likely he had already been plotting a revolt because the next day Ben-hadad was murdered and our writer says Hazael did it.

Such was the intrigue of those confusing times.

The story further confirms, however, that Elisha, the Lord's messenger, was respected and revered because of his integrity. Even his enemies knew that his word from the Lord could be trusted.

Meanwhile in Judah

In order to keep the record straight, the searchlight of Jewish history focuses briefly on Judah (8:16–29). We're told that King Jehoshaphat of Judah was succeeded by his son Jehoram—not the Jehoram or Joram who is listed as a king of Israel. Jehoram of Judah was married to a daughter of Ahab, and in all likelihood she was responsible for leading him away from the faith of his father. In the Book of Chronicles and in secular history it becomes clear that Jehoram was guilty of idolatry and murder.

When Jehoram died, he was succeeded by his son Ahaziah who reigned for only one year and who in the words of our writer "walked in the way of the house of Ahab, and did evil in the sight of the Lord" (8:27). From this we see clearly that things were deteriorating in Judah just as they had in Israel.

Time for a New Start

Under the direction of Elisha, a new character, Jehu, moves from the wings to center stage in Israel's history. As an officer in King Jehoram's army, Jehu was at this time stationed in Ramoth-gilead east of the Jordan River. The action started when Elisha instructed one of his assistants to travel to Ramoth-gilead and anoint Jehu as Israel's next king (9:1).

Elisha gave his assistant detailed instructions. When he arrived at Ramoth-gilead he was to go to the army headquarters and specifically ask for "Jehu the son of Jehoshaphat [not the king] the son of Nimshi." Then he was to request a private meeting. When the two men were alone he was to anoint Jehu with the oil he had brought and give him his commission—Elisha's prophecy on the annihilation of "the house of Ahab," the dynasty of Omri. Then the messenger was to leave immediately (9:2–13).

Everything worked out exactly as anticipated. And when Jehu's fellow officers asked him what the messenger from Elisha had wanted, he told them he had just been anointed as Israel's new king. Now, obviously we don't have the whole story here, only the barest of details. But it becomes immediately apparent that Jehu's news was well received, for they celebrated with the blowing of trumpets and "saying, Jehu is king" (9:13). Some interpreters of these events have suggested there may even have been thought of revolt before then.

A New King in Israel

With the support of his generals and the troops at Ramoth-gilead, Jehu headed northwest to Jezreel where Jehoram (Joram) was recovering from battle wounds and entertaining Ahaziah king of Judah who was paying a state visit (9:14–16). When Jehu and his company—driving furiously (9:20)—arrived in the region of Jezreel, Jehoram was informed. After attempting unsuccessfully through emissaries to find out Jehu's intentions, both King Jehoram (Joram) and

A view of a portion of the Black Obelisk if Shalmaneser. Pictured here is Jehu, king of Israel, bowing at the feet of Shalmaneser, king of Assyria while Jehu's servants present tribute gifts to the Assyrian monarch.

King Ahaziah went out themselves to meet Jehu and his company (9:17–21).

When the king of northern Israel and the king of Judah met General Jehu, it was immediately clear that this was far from a peaceful encounter and mission as Jehu declared bluntly that peace was impossible now because of queen mother Jezebel, her idol worship, and treachery. With that word, the two kings wheeled around in their chariots and headed away at full speed (9:22–23).

The words of the Kings writer described vividly what happened next, "And Jehu drew a bow with his full strength, and smote Jehoram between his arms [shoulders], and the arrow went out at his heart, and he sunk down in his chariot." Jehoram of Israel was dead, and his body was disposed of (9:24–26). Then follows a bloody purge in which Ahaziah of Judah was killed (9:27); the queen mother Jezebel met a miserable death (9:30–37); all of the male descendants and advisors of Ahab were wiped out (10:1–11); and forty-two members of Judah's royal family, the relatives of Ahaziah were slaughtered (10:12–14), along with everyone in Samaria who worshiped Baal (10:18–27).

This was a grisly scene of killing and judgment, and it marked the end of the grossly evil dynasty of Omri. Jehu was faithful in his destruction of Baal worship in Israel; however, we are told that he allowed the golden calves to remain in the shrines at Bethel and Dan, and that he "took no heed to walk in the law of the Lord God of Israel with all his heart" (10:28–31). Following this analysis the Kings writer summarizes the main events of Jehu's reign, which lasted a total of twenty-eight years, in two sentences. Upon his death he was buried in Samaria and succeeded by his son Jehoahaz (10:32–36).

Secular History Speaks of Jehu

Around 840 B.C. Shalmaneser III of Assyria attacked a Syrian coalition which included Israel. Apparently Jehu decided to pay tribute instead of fighting. This action is recorded, along with a likeness of Jehu, on the well-known Black Obelisk of Shalmaneser which was discovered in the royal palace at Nimrud in 1846. A part of the inscription on this obelisk reads, "Tribute of Jehu, son of Omri. Silver, gold, a golden bowl, a golden beaker, golden goblets, pitchers of gold, staves for the hand of the king, javelina, I received from him." It should be noted that while Jehu was not a part of the Omri Dynasty, in those times all of Israel's kings were so classified.

Athaliah and Jehoash (Joash) of Judah

Chapters 11 and 12 of 2 Kings focus on the southern kingdom of Judah. When King Ahaziah was killed by Jehu, his mother Athaliah seized the throne and attempted to destroy any and all who would normally have succeeded Ahaziah (11:1). However, the dead king's sister, Jehosheba, saved one of his young sons—Joash (Jehoash)—and with the help of her husband Jehoiada, a priest, hid the young boy in the temple complex where he was cared for during the few years of the queen's reign (11:2–3).

In the seventh year of Queen Athaliah's reign when Joash was around eight years old, Jehosheba and Jehoiada convinced the priests and Levites and the Temple guard that young Prince Joash should be crowned king. The plot was carefully laid, and as we see in these verses, each participant played the assigned role (11:4–12), and the ceremony ended with everyone present clapping their hands and shouting "God save the king."

When sounds of the celebration reached Queen Athaliah, she hurried to the Temple and saw what was happening. Her personal guards were outnumbered by the assembled Temple guards, so the coup was a success and the wicked and idolatrous queen was executed (11:13–16). The boy king assumed his role and reigned in Judah from approximately 835 to 796 B.C.

With the ascension of Joash to the throne the temples and altars to Baal were destroyed, and the people of Judah looked to the future with joy (11:17–21). While not all of the pagan altars—high places—were destroyed throughout Judah, the forty–year reign of King Joash (Jehoash) was marked by faithfulness to the Lord (12:1–3).

The high point of Joash's rule was his restoration of the Temple in Jerusalem. By this time Solomon's magnificent Temple was almost one hundred and fifty years old and was apparently in dire need of repair. The parallel account of this period in 2 Chronicles 24 tells us also that Queen Athaliah and her sons had desecrated the Temple. But under the leadership of Joash the restoration was completed (12:4–16).

In the closing verses of our Scripture for this lesson the writer picks up the thread given us in Chapter 10:32–33, and tells us that King Hazael of Syria in his southern campaign laid siege to Jerusalem and carried off the Temple treasures (12:17–18). Then follows a sketchy account of the murder of Joash by his servants. This is described in greater detail in 2 Chronicles 24. Finally, we're told that Joash was succeeded by his son Amaziah (12:19–21).

A Lesson for Today

During the period of time involved in our Scripture for this lesson we've witnessed the close of Elijah's ministry, the succession of Elisha as God's spokesman, and the marvelous way he represented the Lord to the people of his day. The contrast between these two prophets helps us see that God uses all kinds of people—the key is having a vision of what God can do with and through people who are obedient to His leading.

We've also moved with breathless speed between northern Israel and southern Judah, which were led by men and women with strange-sounding names. Now and then there were those who "did what was right in the eyes of the Lord," but it seems for the most part the majority rejected the Lord God of Israel, devoted themselves to pagan gods and despicable practices, and followed a brutal lifestyle that we find hard even to read about.

In all of this, we can't help but be deeply moved by the grace and patience of God. The moral and spiritual deterioration of His people of Judah and Israel has followed a steady pattern since the heyday of David and Solomon, but God continues to be patient with them.

At the same time, we find a model for devotion and faith in prophets like Elijah and Elisha and in those kings who "did what was right in the sight of the Lord." These spiritual ancestors of ours prepared the way for us and our pilgrimage of faith by commitment to their God—and ours.

Father, I recommit myself to You fully. Thank you for making me like Jesus. AMEN.

WHAT THIS SCRIPTURE MEANS TO ME
2 Kings 1–12

In the midst of accounts of many of the kings of Israel and Judah and their idolatry and political alliances and battles and intrigues, I was delighted to read about the role that a simple Israelite girl played in Naaman's visit to Elisha. She was a slave who had been assigned as a maid to Naaman's wife. Even though she had been taken captive to another country, she still wished her master to be cured of his leprosy, so she told her mistress about the prophet Elisha in her native land. Because Naaman was an important military leader in Syria, the king sent him to Israel to be healed. After washing in the Jordan River as Elisha instructed, his leprosy disappeared. I am so glad that this unnamed girl wanted to share the good news about God and his prophet with her master. She could easily have been sullen and hostile, and Naaman might never have known about God.

This girl's example makes me realize anew that I don't have to be a preacher or a missionary to pass along God's good news to Sharon at work, to Joan in aerobics class, or to my neighbor Ruth—to the Japanese family who just moved to the United States with Toyota, to members of my own family, or to children I teach in Sunday school. It's good to know that God can use even an unimportant person like me if I am willing!

There is another account in this Scripture lesson about a woman who served God in a different way. We don't know her name, but she lived in Shunem and is referred to as the "Shunammite woman." She was wealthy and had social standing in her community. Her special gift to God was hospitality. She invited the prophet Elisha for meals when he was in the area, and she and her husband even added a guest room to their house for him to use.

For two summers when I was in college I worked as a summer missionary in Georgia, and I still remember with fondness the many people who provided beds and meals for me and the other workers. I am also reminded that one of the reasons I chose to serve as a summer missionary was because of the influence of religious workers whom my parents entertained when they came to our church. As a child I enjoyed their conversation and laughter in fellowship times after church, and it gave me a good impression of ministers as happy people. As an adult, I've invited ministers to our home so that our children could get to know and enjoy them as persons too.

Our Scripture lesson includes many accounts of miracles that Elisha performed as a prophet. Some of them are similar to miracles performed by his teacher Elijah. Before Elijah disappeared into a whirlwind he had asked Elisha what he wanted from him, and Elisha had answered that he wanted "a double portion of thy spirit." Evidently this was his legacy from his teacher.

Elijah's mantle fell on Elisha both literally and figuratively. In reading the stories of what Elisha did, I was interested to see that he always used his special powers for the good of others rather than for himself. Selflessness has always characterized the true servants and prophets of God.

LESSON 6
2 Kings 13–17

On the Road Toward Oblivion

Father, Enable me to do what is right in the sight of the Lord.
AMEN.

For a number of years the great conductor Leonard Bernstein held Saturday morning symphony performances for children. To illustrate a point one day he played four ascending notes and reminded his listeners that these introduced the bar-room ditty entitled, "How Dry I Am." Then he pointed out that these same notes introduced the symphonic tone poem "Death and Transfiguration" by Richard Strauss.

Quite a contrast! But his point is well taken. Life offers us all "the same notes," even as it offers us the choice of the kind of song we can sing. The kind of music we make in the adventure of life depends on the way we use the notes we have.

This has certainly been true in our study so far of the kingdoms of Israel and Judah. It was God's intention for His people to live in their world in tune with His music—"to do what was right in the sight of the Lord." But as time passed, all too often the notes were formed into the wrong music as the people did what was "evil in the sight of the Lord."

Two Minor Kings

Our last lesson ended with the death of Joash of Judah who reigned as king from about 835 to 796 B.C. As we move into Chapter 13 of 2 Kings, the scene shifts to the northern kingdom of Israel, and we have a brief account of two kings—Jehoahaz and Jehoash (13:1–13). The Kings writer tells us that both of these kings "did evil in the sight of the Lord," and both were guilty of "the sins of Jeroboam"—permitting worship of the bull calves. As a matter of fact, before we conclude this lesson we will meet seven more kings of Israel, all of whom did "evil in the sight of the Lord." Someone has jokingly compared this list of kings with the American presidents between Andrew Jackson and Abraham Lincoln.

Jehoahaz of Israel

Jehoahaz was the son of Jehu and reigned for a period of seventeen years (13:1–9). During this time, because of Israel's sin, the Lord allowed them to suffer oppression from Hazael, king of Syria, and his son and successor Ben-hadad (13:3).

Actually, from our point of view it wouldn't be necessary to do anything more than merely mention Jehoahaz, except for one thing. Our writer tells us that because of the Syrian oppression, Jehoahaz and his people repented of their sins and prayed to the Lord for deliverance (13:4). It was an obvious prayer of desperation. As happens so often even today, when the king got to the end of his rope, he turned to God. During World War II we heard a lot about "foxhole religion." There was nothing like being under fire with bullets whizzing overhead to make a soldier think about God and say his prayers.

But the great thing about this story is that the Lord heard the prayers of Jehoahaz and sent a deliverer (13:5–6). We see from this that even in some of Israel's darkest days, the patience and mercy of God were active. He gave the people of Israel another chance by lifting their oppression so they could live in peace for a time—"the children of Israel dwelt in their tents [were at peace]." Then and now God's grace is present in the world. Yes, He is the God of history, but He is also the caring and loving heavenly

Father who responds to the prayers of His people—of each of us.

Jehoash of Israel

As for Jehoash (or Joash), we're told simply that he succeeded his father, that he reigned as king for sixteen years, that he waged a successful war with King Amaziah of Judah (13:12; 14:8–15), and then died and was buried in Samaria. We do, though, pick up a little more information about this period in the story that follows of Elisha's last days and his death.

Elisha's Last Days

We haven't heard anything about Elisha since he anointed Jehu as king over Israel. It is apparent, though, that his influence remained strong, for in this next scene we find the old prophet on his deathbed being visited by King Joash (Jehoash) (13:14–21). Our biblical writer tells us that the king "came down" to visit Elisha. It is generally thought that the king traveled from Samaria to Gilgal, Elisha's boyhood home, to which he had apparently gone to die and be buried. If this is the case, it is a strong testimony as to how important the prophet was to Joash and the people of Israel.

We don't know the full implications of this scene, but it appears likely from the king's actions and the wording that in the face of a depleted army, Elisha, as a prophet of God, was looked upon as Israel's first line of defense against their Syrian enemies. And so we have the king mourning Elisha's impending death and saying in effect, "What are we going to do now?"

In response to that question, Elisha decides to give the king an object lesson. Elisha tells King Joash to take his bow and a quiver of arrows and shoot them out of an east window in the direction of Syria. The reading in our King James text is a bit obscure, but it seems that Elisha wanted the king to shoot all the arrows out the window where they would ultimately fall to the ground.

Our Kings writer then tells us that Joash shot three arrows out the window and then stopped. And with that we see an angry and disappointed prophet as he says, "Thou shouldest have smitten five or six times; then hadst thou smitten Syria till thou hadst consumed it: whereas now thou shalt smite Syria but

121

thrice" (13:19). In other words Elisha had intended for the king to shoot all of the arrows in his quiver, but he stopped too soon. Joash's action became a symbol of the nation's future; instead of a complete victory over Syria they would enjoy just a partial victory.

The meaning of this object lesson for King Joash certainly applies just as readily to our Christian pilgrimage. We, like Joash, often stop too soon in our spiritual life and endeavors. Our Lord intends for us to persist in our growth and development as Christians, but we give up so easily and miss the full victory He intends for us to enjoy.

The Apostle Paul exhibited the kind of passion Elisha was looking for in this story—a single-minded determination to share in the full experience God intends for His people. We catch Paul's feeling of urgency as he wrote to his Christian friends at Philippi, "Brethren, I count not myself to have apprehended [I haven't arrived yet]: but this one thing I do, forgetting those things which are behind, and reaching forth unto those things which are before, I press toward the mark for the prize of the high calling of God in Christ Jesus" (Phil. 3:13–14).

The Death of a Prophet

Earlier we witnessed the dramatic passing of Elijah as he was caught up in a chariot of fire and whirlwind east of the Jordan River. Of Elisha our writer says simply, "And Elisha died, and they buried him" (13:20a). There was no razzle-dazzle in Elisha's passing off the scene, but his had been a powerful witness. The miracle events of his life and ministry gave ample proof that God was with him. His gifts were different from Elijah's, but he served his Lord faithfully.

To some, the Lord gives the gift of leadership; to others, the gift of being a faithful follower. Some Christians witness center stage under the glare of lights. Other "quiet Christians" serve behind the scenes but use their full quiver of arrows and hang in resolutely until the job is done. God moves and acts through Elijah-Christians and through Elisha-Christians. Both are commended for faithful service.

Life after Death

Our writer closes out the Elisha drama with a strange and unusual miracle story (13:20–21). Some time after Elisha's death and burial, just as a funeral was being held for an unnamed man, a band of Moabite raiders appeared on the scene. The funeral party had to act quickly to get out of the raiders' way, so they pushed the body into the first available sepulcher—Elisha's. When the corpse touched Elisha's remains, the storyteller writes, "he [the corpse] revived, and stood up on his feet" (13:21b).

As you would expect, there have been various and sundry explanations for this, Elisha's capstone miracle. Explanations are best left with the Lord. The important message for us in all of this is to know that in life and in death God uses the witness of His faithful people in marvelous and often miraculous ways.

Elisha's Prophecy Is Fulfilled

As we have seen, the pressure of Syria was constantly felt in Israel. But now, because of growing Assyrian pressure on Syria (a fact gained from secular history), Israel was able, in spite of its smaller army, to win partial victory over Ben-hadad of Syria and regain possession of the cities east of the Jordan that King Hazael had captured. Notice the wording, "Three times did Joash beat him [Ben-hadad], and recovered the cities of Israel" (13:25). Joash won three victories over the Syrians—the same number of arrows he shot from the east window of Elisha's home. It was a partial victory, just as Elisha had predicted.

Meanwhile in Judah

Once again the Kings writer switches from the northern kingdom to the south in order to give us the complete story of the Jewish people. The southern kingdom of Judah is now under the leadership of Amaziah who ruled as king for twenty-nine years in Jerusalem (14:1–22). Amaziah, one of the stronger kings of Judah, is characterized as one who "did that which was right in the sight of the Lord" (14:3). But the endorsement is a qualified one, because he allowed "the high places"—the pagan altars—to re-

main and be used for the worship of the Lord. He
seems to be best known for his success in waging war
against Edom and for his defeat by the armies of
Israel.

Judah's Success in Edom

Throughout all of Old Testament history the Hebrews and the Edomites were deadly enemies. The
Edomites were the descendants of Esau and lived in
the desert wilderness, the valley of salt referred to in
14:7, south of the Dead Sea. *Selah*, also mentioned in
verse 7, means "rock" and probably refers to Petra,
the capital city of Edom, which was carved out of the
cliffs of a hidden valley. The description of the Edom
campaign here is quite brief, but we learn more about
it in 2 Chronicles 25. There we discover that Amaziah
employed the services of some soldiers from Israel to
bolster his own army.

*The vicinity of Petra in Edom. It was in country like this
that King Amaziah won his decisive victory over the
Edomites (2 Kings 14; 2 Chronicles 25).*

Judah Defeated by Israel

Fresh from his victory in Edom King Amaziah made some threatening gestures toward the northern kingdom of Israel. Jehoash of Israel tried to reason with him with a rather neat little story about a little thistle thinking itself on a par with a big cedar (14:9–10). Amaziah should have taken the hint and backed down, but he didn't. The two armies were locked in battle at Beth-shemesh, Judah was badly defeated, and Amaziah taken captive (14:11–13a).

Then to add insult to injury the army of Israel tore down two hundred yards of the walls of Jerusalem, carried off the gold and valuables of the Temple, and emptied the treasury. They returned home leaving Judah bankrupt (14:12–14 and 2 Chron. 25).

Over-confidence has always been dangerous. Most certainly, Amaziah, after his successes in Edom, had an exaggerated sense of his own importance. But this time Israel put him in his place. In 2 Chronicles 25:14–16 we get another clue as to the reason for the defeat—apparently Amaziah and the people of Judah had taken to worshiping the Edomite idols they had captured and were being punished for their idolatry.

Amaziah continued to rule in Jerusalem for another fifteen or twenty years. Eventually he was assasinated and was succeeded by his son Azariah (Uzziah) (14:18–22).

Jeroboam II

Once again, briefly, the scene shifts to the northern kingdom, where Jeroboam II succeeds his father Joash (Jehoash) as king of Israel (14:23–29). Jeroboam II reigned as king for forty-one years and achieved unusual success and prosperity. Yet, the cutting description of Jeroboam II reveals his true character, "He did that which was evil in the sight of the Lord: he departed not from all the sins of Jeroboam the son of Nebat, who made Israel to sin" (14:24).

The biblical record of the reign of Jeroboam II is sparse, in spite of the length of his rule and his military and economic successes. Our writer viewed Jeroboam's time from God's perspective. Political, social, and economic success is not the way God measures the worth of people. It is obedience to Him that matters.

The Greatest since David and Solomon

Our fast-moving history lesson continues with a brief look at the reign of Azariah (Uzziah) in Judah. In cryptic language we're told that he reigned as king in Jerusalem for fifty-two years and that "he did that which was right in the sight of the Lord" (15:1–3). He was one of the four kings of Judah who ranked as heroes with our writers. The other three were Jehoshaphat, Hezekiah, and Josiah. The Chronicles writer (Chapter 26) expands a bit on our information by telling us that these were prosperous years, that Azariah was successful in military efforts, and that he rebuilt the walls of Jerusalem. Beyond that we're told that he had leprosy and that he died and was buried in "the city of David" (15:4–7).

Dark and Evil Days in Israel

Very briefly now the Kings writer parades the names of six kings of Israel across a very few verses of our Scripture lesson (15:8–31). Jeroboam II was succeeded by his son Zechariah, who reigned for only six months. As the fourth generation of the Jehu dynasty, his short rule fulfilled the promise God had made to Jehu that his sons would rule Israel through the fourth generation (10:30). The Lord fulfilled His promise even though Zechariah "did that which was evil in the sight of the Lord" (15:9). In this, as always, we see that in spite of our failures God can always be counted on because He keeps His promises.

The stability gained by Jeroboam II did not last. Zechariah was assassinated by Shallum, who only lasted one month. He was murdered by Menahem, who then reigned as king in Samaria for ten years. It was during this time that Israel became a vassal state to Assyria. The tribute money Menahem paid to Assyria and King Pul or Tiglath-pileser III would be equivalent to more than four million dollars and he raised it by taxing the wealthy citizens of Israel (15:8–20).

Menahem was followed by the two-year reign of his son Pekahiah who was murdered in a revolt led by Pekah (15:27–29). During Pekah's twenty-year reign Assyria ravaged much of Israel, reducing the northern kingdom to a relatively small area and taking many Jews back to Assyria as captives (c. 733 B.C.).

The sordid story of the deterioration of the northern kingdom of Israel is moving now toward its fatal climax. The Kings writer draws down the curtain on the reign of Pekah by telling us that another bloody revolt was staged, this time by Hoshea, who murdered Pekah and usurped the throne. The writer's epitaph for each of Israel's kings is the same: "they did that which was evil in the sight of the Lord." Rejection of God and idolatry of the grossest nature had the nation of Israel on the skids. Centuries later the Apostle Paul, in his letter to the Christians at Rome, spelled out the consequences clearly when he wrote, "For the wages of sin is death" (Rom. 6:23). The moment of truth was near when Hoshea assumed the throne—death and destruction were lurking just around the corner.

Another Look at Judah

After the long reign of King Azariah (Uzziah) in Judah, he was succeeded by his son Jotham (15:32–37). We know virtually nothing about him except that he rebuilt or repaired the "higher [upper] gate of the house of the Lord [the Temple]" that "he did that which was right in the sight of the Lord except for not removing the high places" (15:34–35), and that he died and was buried in the city of David (15:38).

The Chronicles writer adds a little to this picture. Jotham built cities and castles and towers and was successful in a war with the Ammonites (2 Chron. 27:1–9). This same writer credits him with being "mighty, because he prepared his ways before the Lord his God." This is further affirmation of his faithfulness and success.

But then the tide turns as Ahaz succeeds his father (2 Kings 16:1–20). Early in the Ahaz story the Kings writer describes him this way, he "did not that which was right in the sight of the Lord" (16:2). Unlike his father and grandfather, Ahaz rejected the worship of God in favor of worshiping the pagan Canaanite gods—he was even guilty of sacrificing his own son by fire on the altar of Molech (16:3–4).

It was a terrifying time in Judah. The Edomites

from the southeast were making raids on cities and countryside, carrying away captives for the slave markets. The Philistines were harassing the inhabitants in the southwest. And in the north, Syria, in league with the kingdom of Israel, was moving south on the attack.

With border cities gobbled up by Judah's enemies, and the port city of Elath on the Gulf of Aqabah lost to Syria, Jerusalem stood in terrifying isolation. The prophet Isaiah described it as a "besieged city" (Isa. 1:8). And now powerful and ruthless Assyria in the northeast was threatening the whole area—Syria, Israel and Judah. Ahaz was in bad trouble.

According to the Chronicles writer, after a disastrous defeat in battle by Syria and Israel (2 Chron. 28), Ahaz made a calculated move to save his own skin. He appealed to Tiglath-pileser, king of Assyria, to protect him. In doing so, he ignored the prophet Isaiah's advice (Isa. 7:1–11), a further instance of his unwillingness to listen to the voice of God. Isaiah told Ahaz bluntly, "If ye will not believe [will not have faith], surely ye shall not be established [you will not be secure]" (Isa. 7:9).

To seal his pact with Assyria, Ahaz stripped the Temple in Jerusalem of its treasures and gave them as tribute to Tiglath-pileser, who went on to defeat the army of Syria under King Resin. After that battle, Ahaz traveled north to Damascus to greet his new master. While there he saw an Assyrian altar of such a beautiful design that he had a model made of it and then built an exact replica and installed it in the Jerusalem Temple (16:10–13).

The reign of King Ahaz signaled dark days for the southern kingdom of Judah as he corrupted the Temple worship with innovations of his own design (16:14–18). Now, the Kings writer drops the curtain on these evil and bloody days by simply saying, "And Ahaz slept with his fathers, and was buried with his fathers in the city of David" (16:20).

King Hoshea and the Defeat of Israel

Once again the Kings writer shifts the scene as the action moves north to Samaria and Israel. Hoshea was now king after having staged a coup and murdering his predecessor. It is said of this nineteenth and last king of Israel that "he did that which was evil in the sight of the Lord, *but not as the kings of Israel that were before him*" (17:2, italics mine). We aren't told why he was better than the others, but we do know that it was during his reign that the Lord's final judgment fell on the northern kingdom. As we shall see, there were ample warnings, but the people and their leaders refused to turn away from their sin. Now, the consequences of their disobedience and idolatry would come in destruction and exile.

In Assyria Shalmaneser had succeeded his father as king. Hoshea became his vassal, and he continued to keep the pressure on Israel and collect tribute money. King Hoshea, however, tried to undercut Shalmaneser by forming an alliance with the king of Egypt. And when Shalmaneser heard about it, he launched an attack on the capital city of Samaria and laid siege to it for three years (17:3–5).

Ultimately, under Sargon II, who succeeded his brother Shalmaneser when he died, Samaria was taken, Hoshea was captured and put in prison, and the people of Israel were transported as exiles to Assyria (17:6). From secular sources we know that Samaria was captured in 722 B.C. and that Sargon boasted that he carried away approximately twenty-seven thousand people into exile, leaving only a handful of people behind to care for the land. We also know that Sargon allowed foreign nationals to settle in Israel (17:24).

The Wages of Sin

Through our study so far we have lived out a history lesson focused on God's chosen people, moving back and forth between the northern kingdom of Israel and the southern kingdom of Judah. From the division of Israel after Solomon's death, it has for the most part been a sad story.

In this next part of our Scripture lesson our writer explains why judgment in the form of complete defeat and exile was inevitable (17:7–12). The people had turned against the God who freed them from Egyptian slavery. They had built pagan altars and had worshiped Canaanite gods and goddesses. In their rejection of God and their worship of false gods, they were guilty of the grossest of sins (17:13–23).

Their basic sin was idolatry—a sin that still plagues society today as we replace the Creator-God with the "respectable" twentieth-century idols of materialism, success, and position.

The Prophets and Seers

Throughout Hebrew history from the earliest times, the real heroes were the prophets—those men and women of God who warned against sin. Now the Kings writer, after having spelled out the reason for Israel's fall, reminds his readers of the faithful prophets who warned of danger. "Yet the Lord testified against Israel, and against Judah, by all the prophets, and by all the seers, saying, Turn ye from your evil ways, and keep my commandments and my statutes, according to all the law which I commanded your fathers, and which I sent to you by my servants the prophets" (17:13).

To read this amazing story is to marvel at God's patience and mercy. Both in Israel's glorious days and in its dark days, God's spokespersons had been faithful in getting His word out. The people of Israel had had their chance to hear and obey, but they persisted in sin. And now the consequences of their disobedience had to be faced.

The Eighth-Century Prophets

During this period we have been studying the active prophets have had familiar names—Joel, Jonah, Obadiah, Isaiah, Micah, Amos, and Hosea. Two of these in particular deserve our attention at this time—Amos, who prophesied in the northern kingdom of Israel, and Isaiah, who ministered in the southern kingdom of Judah.

It is important to understand that prophets were God's spokesmen for their own times as well as for the future. They were called of God to speak for Him. They were "forthtellers" of God's word as well as "foretellers."

Amos

Amos, the first of the writing prophets, prophesied around 750 B.C., in the northern kingdom of Israel during the reign of Jeroboam II. It was at this same time that Azariah (Uzziah) was king of the southern kingdom of Judah.

Amos was actually a native of Judah, from the

town of Tekoa, a two hour donkey ride several miles southeast of Bethlehem in a rocky and barren land. Before he traveled north from Judah to prophesy in Israel, Amos, by his own admission, was not a prophet or a son of a prophet, but was a herdsman who also looked after sycamore trees (Amos 1:1; 7:14–15). But he knew right from wrong, and he was sensitive to the voice of the Lord.

Amos spoke out sharply against social injustice and exploitation of the poor. His message is pregnant with passionate calls to repentance.

There was nothing parochial about Amos. He was well versed in conditions in Syria to the north (Amos 1:3–5), in Edom to the south (Amos 1:11–12), in the Philistine cities of the southwest (Amos 1:6–8), in the Phoenician seaport of Tyre in the northwest (Amos 1:9–10), and with Ammon and Moab, east of the Jordan River (Amos 1:13–2:3). Amos also spoke out against the sinful activities and callous attitudes of Judah and Israel. He denounced Israel's sins and warned of future punishment as a consequence of their rejection of God.

For the people of his time, Amos interpreted events with authority. He prefaced his preaching with "Thus saith the Lord," "Hear this word that the Lord hath spoken," and "the Lord said unto me." In many ways Amos could be considered a prophet of doom as he spoke out against sin and predicted judgment. At the same time, though, he was a prophet of hope. He called the people to seek God and live (Amos 5:4), and in the closing paragraphs of his book he looks into the future and sees the restoration of Israel and the rebuilding of its cities (Amos 9:11–15). In truth, Amos was a "man of God" and a "messenger of the Lord."

Isaiah

The other eighth-century B.C. prophet I want to profile briefly is Isaiah. He was active in the southern kingdom of Judah for more than forty years during the time of King Azariah (Uzziah), 783–742 B.C.; King Jotham, 742–735 B.C.; King Ahaz, 735–715 B.C.; and King Hezekiah, 715–687 B.C. (Isa. 1:1).

It is thought that Isaiah was a member of the royal family of Judah. From his prophecies we discover that he was a man of wisdom, a statesman, an eloquent and accomplished speaker and writer. He was married and had two sons. Like Amos, Isaiah had a vision of God. With strong yet poetic language he spoke out against the oppression and exploitation of the poor and against any involvement, political or social, that compromised Judah's relationship with the Lord.

Isaiah saw God as the Lord of all history and as the One who is high and holy—a moral God who demands purity and social justice from His people. He is known as the prophet of righteousness—a word used fifty-eight times in the Book of Isaiah.

The End of the Northern Kingdom of Israel

Before going on, stop a moment and reread verses 7 through 17 of 2 Kings 17. These verses show that the people of the northern kingdom of Israel were guilty of just about every crime and sin in the book, including child sacrifice and witchcraft. They had rejected the Lord. Now, the Kings writer tells us, the Lord has rejected them (17:18–23).

In exacting judgment on the people of the northern kingdom of Israel, the Lord permitted the king of Assyria, probably Sargon II, to completely overwhelm the nation. A large segment of the population was transported into exile in the various cities and centers of Assyria. At the same time Sargon moved settlers from different parts of the Assyrian empire into Samaria, the name now given to the entire area (17:24–28). This mixture of races and people eventually wiped out any separate racial and religious identities.

To the pantheon of Canaanite gods which had corrupted the worship of the people, the new settlers from the east brought their own gods (17:29–31). Mentioned in this part of our Scripture lesson are the Babylonian god Succoth-benoth, said to resemble a hen and chickens, and Nergal, the Babylonian god of the underworld and a war god comparable to the Roman god Mars. We know little about Ashima except that it was reported to look like a hairless goat. Nibhaz had the form of a dog and Tartak had the appearance of a donkey. The other two gods mentioned in verse 31 were evidently Mesopotamian deities.

This weird assortment of deities mixed with the worship of God made for a grotesque religious environment (17:32–34) that was in direct violation of the covenant God had made with the Hebrew people, "Ye shall not fear other gods, nor bow yourselves to them, nor serve them, nor sacrifice to them" (17:35).

With the fall of the northern kingdom of Israel, now referred to as Samaria, the exile of large numbers of its population, and the corruption and absorption of the Hebrew people left in Samaria by the new settlers, the identity of the ten northern tribes of Israel was lost for all time. The year 722 B.C. was a tragic one in the history of the Hebrew people. For generations God had been patient and merciful as through the prophets and certain righteous kings He had attempted to stop the flow of evil and corruption that stained Hebrew life.

But the people persisted in their disobedience until now the inevitable happened—the consequences of their sin had to be paid. God had made it clear through the Law given to Moses on Mount Sinai that He was a "jealous God" who, in the end, would not tolerate the people's rejection and sinful practices.

A Severe Judgment?

As we have viewed the deterioration of the once great nation of Israel from its golden years under David and Solomon, we cannot help but be aware of the persistent hints and threats of judgment. Throughout this tragic story we see God at work among the people as He tries to win them back to Himself and stop the senseless plunge into idolatry with all of the baggage that goes with it.

At the same time, the theme that runs persistently through the drama of both the southern kingdom of Judah and the northern kingdom of Israel is the patience and mercy and grace of God. Yes, the northern kingdom of Israel finally had to pay the consequence of its persistent and headlong disobedience. There was no escape then, even as there is no escape now in the late twentieth century for stubborn disobedience. But throughout His story then and now, there is a vibrant note of hope. This dark chapter in the history of the Hebrew people was not the last.

In a similar way our twentieth-century life reflects a pattern of idolatry as we bow before the gods of materialism, space- and microtechnology, political and social status, and cheap grace. At the same time, there is a weakening of moral and ethical standards. Though the outward forms and shapes are different, we cannot ignore the inner parallels between our day and Israel and Judah of the eighth century B.C.

But for them and for us, judgment is not the last word. A century after the Assyrians gutted Israel, another prophet wrote, "And there is hope in thine end, saith the Lord, that thy children shall come again to their own border" (Jer. 31:17). And this side of the Cross and the Resurrection, Christians have the words of the great Apostle who wrote, "Christ in you, the hope of glory" (Col. 1:27).

God is still in charge!

Master, I am glad You are in charge—not only of my life, but the entire world is subject to Your beautiful sovereignty. How relieving it is to know I can fully trust You. AMEN.

WHAT THIS SCRIPTURE MEANS TO ME
2 Kings 13—17

On a January afternoon several years ago while on a tour of the Holy Land, I visited the hill of Samaria which used to be the capital of the Northern Kingdom of Israel. The guide told us of Ahab's "ivory palaces" that had graced the summit. He let us walk up the roadbed to the top—a road that had been wide enough for several chariots to pass each other at the same time. But when I reached the crest of the hill, all I saw were booths where peddlers were selling souvenirs to the tourists. And the only things along the roadbed that reminded me of its former splendor were remnants of small mosaic tiles.

I thought of that day as I read over and over again in these chapters the words describing the kings of Israel that they "did that which was evil in the sight of the Lord." And I wondered about the connection between the desolate capital hill and the choices of its leaders to "do evil."

Often when bad things happen to us they are not of our own making—an unavoidable illness, a child hit by a drunken driver, an economic crunch, or situations we are caught in because of bad decisions by others. But there are times when our choices to "do evil" affect us directly with disastrous results that have a "domino" effect through the years—a husband or wife who chooses not to be faithful; a business partner who chooses not to be honest; a lie that is told about someone; not making time for God in our lives.

I can't just say, "So what! It's *my* business!" The choices I make affect me—but they also affect others. And I wouldn't like to look ahead through my years and see a desolate hill of Samaria where once there had been ivory palaces. I wouldn't want it said of me that I "did evil in the sight of the Lord."

It seems that many of the kings of Israel and Judah thought they could worship God and Baal at the same time. We may think it was foolish of them to suppose that they could do this. But is it so unusual? We can be just as influenced by things happening in our culture as they were in theirs. It is still possible to pay lip service to God and be caught up in the mores of the times in which we live.

I may say that I want to serve God, but I also want to live my own life and do what everyone else is doing. When I accept their actions as my model, I find it hard to make the distinction between what is godly and what is not. I have some of the same problems the children of Israel had when they tried to worship God and the local pagan gods at the same time.

But even in the midst of the account of so many generations in Israel and Judah that didn't choose to obey God, we still see that God didn't give up on them. And He doesn't give up on us either! He still loves us and wants us to repent and return to Him. What a marvelous hope for imperfect me!

LESSON 7
2 Kings 18–25

The End of the Line

Master, It is truly wonderful to know You, to have faith in You, to believe and love You. Thank You for the privilege of salvation. AMEN.

The final chapters of 2 Kings which make up our Scripture lesson give us a vivid picture of the fall of the southern kingdom of Judah. In this picture we are able to see the crucial distinction between the Judeo-Christian faith and most other faiths. We have here a story about faith *in* Someone (God)—and, only secondarily faith *that* something is true. As an astronaut is supposed to have remarked about the Johnson Space Center in Houston, to have faith *in* "those guys back in Houston" cuts more ice than simply having faith that the instruments in the space capsule will function properly.

Faith *in someone* describes a continually growing relationship. This simply means that having faith in a God we know in a personal way matters much more than having faith in a philosophical world view. From this perspective then, it is not that I believe something to be true. Rather it is that "I believe you." It is not an arrangement of knowledge but confidence and trust in God.

The Last Days

Steadily now we will be moving along over the years to that moment when the curtain falls on the southern kingdom of Judah (587 B.C.). Ironically, the very people who believe in God often commit idolatry in the name of God, and we see this occurring during this period of national decline. The people of Judah boasted, in effect, "We are immune from trouble. We are God's people, living in God's country, worshiping in God's Temple, and living under God's protection. Therefore it doesn't matter how we live or what other gods we worship." They could look back to the days of King Hezekiah when the Assyrians had threatened to wipe them out but didn't, and therefore they said, "Nothing happened then. Why should we worry now? God is good; everything will be all right."

But in response to such attitudes God sent His prophets to warn the rulers and people of Judah that their sins were moving them steadily toward the kind of doom that struck the northern kingdom of Israel.

King Hezekiah of Judah

Somewhere between 729 and 715 B.C. Hezekiah, the son of Ahaz, was crowned king of Judah. As our Kings writer picks up on the story we're immediately told three things: (1) the new king was twenty-five years old when he was crowned, (2) he reigned as king for twenty-nine years, and (3) "he did that which was right in the sight of the Lord" (18:1–3).

Hezekiah was a renaissance man. He could do many things well. As a civil engineer he directed the construction of a tunnel 1,708 feet long through solid limestone so water could be brought into the city from a spring outside the walls (2 Chron. 32:30). He was also a patron of music and literature. His interest in Solomon's proverbs is referred to in the Book of Proverbs (Ch. 25), and the prophet Isaiah records a beautiful song written by Hezekiah (Isa. 38:9–20). He was a versatile, unusual man—he could write a poem, design a water system, lead in prayer—and do it all with style and skill.

Right at the beginning of his reign, Hezekiah took positive steps to rekindle faith in God among his people. And as a first step he completely destroyed the pagan altars and the "high places" that were used in the degrading worship of the Canaanite gods (18:3). A further step he took involves a surprising fact. Apparently the brass serpent that was fashioned by Moses during the Hebrews' forty years in the wilderness had been preserved (the original story is in Numbers 21). With the passing of the centuries this brass serpent had apparently become sort of an idol and was worshiped by the people.

Now we read that in addition to destroying all of the Canaanite altars and symbols, Hezekiah broke up the brass serpent (18:4). When Moses had fashioned it, it was as an instrument of healing. But what had once been good was no longer

Hezekiah's Religious Reform

The assault ramp built by Assyrian king Sennacherib at Lachish. The Assyrians destroyed the city in 701 B.C. (2 Kings 18:17–37).

A Bas relief carving taken from the palace of Sennacherib in Nineveh recording and celebrating the capture of Lachish.

useful and had become an object of worship. It had to go, and it did.

The Kings writer is lavish in his praise of Hezekiah's religious zeal (18:5–6). And the Chronicles writer adds to the story by telling us that he re-opened the doors of the Temple and restored worship of the Lord, including observance of the Passover festival (2 Chron. 29–30).

A National Crisis

Suddenly, however, Hezekiah found his country in grave danger. The mighty Assyrian army had marched into Judah and was threatening Jerusalem (18:13–19:37). For years Hezekiah had been advised to link up with either Assyria or Egypt for protection, and now here he was being besieged by the Assyrian hordes (18:13).

In an effort to head off trouble Hezekiah agreed to pay King Sennacherib of Assyria an assessment of silver and gold that would amount to approximately four million dollars according to today's value (18:14–16).

But this payment of tribute didn't buy peace, for we next have a picture of a large force of the Assyrian army moving right up to the walls of Jerusalem, along with a delegation from Sennacherib, "Tartan and Rabsaris and Rab-shakeh" to negotiate with Hezekiah (18:17). In the King James text it would appear that these are the proper names of the men who made up the delegation. But later scholarship and translation indicate that the names are actually titles like commander-in-chief, chief of staff, etc.

In response to the Assyrian delegation's request for a negotiating session, King Hezekiah selected three top-level ambassadors of his own to participate in the discussions. Then comes a somewhat humorous exchange, not unlike some of our twentieth-century diplomatic doubletalk. Boiled down to its simplest form, the Assyrian ambassador said, in effect, "Tell your king I'll give you two thousand horses if you can supply enough men to ride them."

Apparently Assyrian intelligence had already penetrated the Jerusalem defenses, because the enemy knew there weren't two thousand able-bodied horsemen available in Jerusalem. Sennacherib's arrogant challenge to Hezekiah (18:19–25) seems to indicate that the Assyrians were familiar with at least some of Isaiah's prophecies which called on Hezekiah to trust in God, not in foreign powers (Isa. 31–33).

Picture the scene if you will. The three Assyrian ambassadors are standing outside the wall of Jerusalem shouting terms in Hebrew to Hezekiah's representatives who are up on the wall. There was no such thing as private diplomacy here; everyone within earshot could understand the bargaining. To offset this, Hezekiah's representatives suggested they converse in Syrian (Aramaic), the language of diplomacy in the ancient Near East. This way the public would not be aware of what was being said (18:26).

The Assyrian ambassadors however refused to comply with diplomatic niceties as they shouted out surrender terms that would have, on the surface, sounded attractive to the people listening (18:27–35). But the Assyrian ploy didn't work. In spite of the fact that the Jews knew about all of the Assyrian victories and the way they had prospered, and in spite of the attractive offers of peace (18:29–35), the people of Jerusalem didn't cave in. They weren't overwhelmed by the terror of the situation, but in response to the request of their king, they "held their peace" and stood firm (18:36). It may be in that critical moment their thoughts went back over the years to the climactic confrontation between the Philistine giant Goliath and David, the shepherd boy from Bethlehem. This doesn't mean that either Hezekiah or his representatives were oblivious to the seriousness of the situation (18:37–19:1), for we're next told that the king turned to Isaiah the prophet, and asked what they should do now (19:2–7).

A Look at Isaiah

Even though Isaiah had been on the scene for a long time—actually since before the death of Hezekiah's grandfather Ahaziah (Uzziah)—this is the first time he is mentioned by the Kings writer. But the old prophet had been well prepared for this moment. In the sixth chapter of the Book of Isaiah we have the amazing and awesome story of Isaiah's early vision of God in the Temple. He had never forgotten the awesome presence of God on that occasion, and he had never forgotten the words of the Lord he heard then.

For Isaiah, the might and power of Sennacherib and his Assyrian army couldn't hold a candle to the might and power of Judah's holy Creator-God. It was this Isaiah who now said, "Thus saith the Lord, Be not afraid of the words which thou hast heard, with which the servants of the king of Assyria have blasphemed me. Behold, I will send a blast upon him [put a spirit in him], and he shall hear a rumour, and shall return to his own land; and I will cause him to fall by the sword in his own land" (19:6–7). Isaiah's faith and trust in God give us a model for our time as well.

Sennacherib's Threat

When Sennacherib's ambassadors returned to Lachish where the Assyrian army had been camped, they discovered that the Assyrian forces had left and were attacking the military stronghold of Libnah. When they caught up with Sennacherib, they reported Hezekiah's stubbornness to him. Upon receiving the report of the Jerusalem conversations, Sennacherib wrote a threatening letter to king Hezekiah and sent it by way of messenger (19:8–13).

Hezekiah Consults the Lord

This time when Hezekiah read the letter from the mighty king of Assyria, he personally went to the Temple to consult with the Lord. His was an impassioned prayer and concludes with these words, "O Lord our God, I beseech thee, save thou us out of his [Sennacherib's] hand, that all the kingdoms of the earth may know that thou art the Lord God, even thou only" (19:19).

Assurance from the Prophet

The Kings writer next tells us that Isaiah sent word to Hezekiah that the Lord had revealed to him the answer to the king's prayer (19:20–34). The word from the Lord through Isaiah takes the form of a poem that is full of picture language. Hezekiah is assured that in spite of Sennacherib's successes in other fields of battle he would not now prevail over Jerusalem. The poem ends with the Lord's promise, "I will defend this city, to save it, *for mine own sake,* and for my servant David's sake" (19:34, italics mine).

What a marvelous word of reassurance Hezekiah and the people of Judah had from the Lord through Isaiah the prophet! For now at least, Jerusalem and the southern kingdom of Judah were safe from the Assyrian forces—not because of anything they had done but through the Lord's intervention.

The Promise Fulfilled

In cryptic language and with a minimum of detail the writer next tells us that "the angel of the Lord" intervened, Sennacherib's army was decimated, and he headed back to his capital city of Nineveh. Sometime after his return to Nineveh he was murdered by two of his sons who, we're told, "escaped into the land of Armenia." Other translations tell us they made their escape to the "land of Ararat"—a mountainous region in Armenia (19:36–37).

143

King Hezekiah's Sickness and Healing

In relating this next episode, the Kings writer apparently goes back in time a few years—probably around the middle of Hezekiah's reign—and gives us the story of Hezekiah's illness and his miraculous healing (20:1–11). Evidently the king had some kind of skin inflammation which had reached an advanced stage, because our writer describes his condition as being "sick unto death."

Isaiah appeared on the scene and informed Hezekiah that he should put his house in order because he was going to die. It isn't hard to imagine the king's feeling of desperation. Immediately he went into seclusion—"turned his face to the wall"—and shut out the rest of the world so he could pray. In verse 3 we have Hezekiah's impassioned prayer.

The Lord acted quickly because Isaiah had not been long gone before the Lord spoke to him and gave him a message for the king (20:4–6). The prophet then returned to the king's bedroom, told him to apply a fig poultice to the infected area, and in due time he would recover. When Hezekiah, in his weakened condition, asked Isaiah for some kind of sign that he would be healed and free of the immediate Assyrian threat, the Lord responded by moving "the shadow ten degrees backward" on the sundial (20:11). A miracle occurred—in some way God had moved the shadow back on the sundial and Hezekiah was healed as the Lord had promised.

Hezekiah's Last Days

At some point following Hezekiah's recovery, the king of Babylon sent letters and envoys to Judah, presumably as a gesture of friendship. In referring to this incident the Chronicles writer in the parallel version of Hezekiah's period (2 Chron. 30–32) indicates that the Babylonian king was apparently also curious about the report he had heard of Hezekiah's miraculous recovery.

It would appear that Hezekiah went overboard in welcoming his Babylonian guests, and let them see all of Israel's treasures and resources, including the armament arsenal. Evidently, the king was trying to really impress his visitors with Judah's material wealth and resources (20:12–13) instead of with their spiritual treasures.

When Isaiah heard what Hezekiah had done, he was deeply disturbed over the king's foolishness. And it was then that Isaiah predicted the coming fall of Judah and destruction of Jerusalem—by none other than the king of Babylon and his army (20:14–18)—a prediction that came true in just a few years.

From Good to Bad

The closing two verses in this part of our Scripture lesson (20:20–21) make reference to Hezekiah's primary engineering accomplishment—"he made the pool and the conduit and brought water into the city." Today's visitor to Jerusalem can walk through that very tunnel which archaeologists uncovered in 1880. And finally, our writer tells us that this amazing king "slept with his fathers: and Manasseh his son reigned in his stead."

While it isn't mentioned here, the Chronicles writer adds that "they buried him in the chiefest of the sepulchres of the sons of David: and all Judah and the inhabitants of Jerusalem did him honour at his death" (2 Chron. 32:33).

If Hezekiah was one of the best of Judah's kings, his son Manasseh was certainly one of the worst (21:1–18). The Kings writer tells us that he reigned as king in Jerusalem for fifty-five years, and that "he did evil in the sight of the Lord." Then follows a list of his sins. He rebuilt the pagan altars his father had torn down. He erected altars to the sun, moon, and stars, and was guilty of sacrificing his own son on the fiery altar of Molech. He dabbled in witchcraft and fortune telling, and was involved in more disgusting and degrading practices than even the pagan Canaanites.

Furthermore, we're told that not only was this king guilty of the grossest of actions himself, but he led the people of Judah into sin as well. Finally his long and wicked reign came to an end with his death, and instead of being accorded the honor of burial in the tombs of the kings, he "was buried in the garden of his own house" (21:18).

Like Father, Like Son

To keep our history straight we'll just mention briefly the two year reign of Amon, Manasseh's son (21:19–26). It is little wonder that this young man, raised as he was in his father's house, "walked in all the way that his father walked in" and did that which was evil. His short reign was ended when he was assassinated, and he, too, was buried in a garden.

Young Josiah Is Crowned King

Following the horrendous regimes of his grandfather Manasseh and his father Amon, Josiah came on like the last burst of light before sunset and darkness. Josiah was only eight years old when he ascended to the throne of Judah in 638 B.C., and for the next eighteen years he reigned under the guidance of

An excavated fort at Uza which was built under King Manasseh about 650 B.C. to fortify the southern border of Judah. Uza is located between twenty and twenty-five miles south of Hebron. This excavation was headed by Dr. Bruce Cresson of Baylor University and was completed in June of 1988. Dr. Cresson took most of the pictures used in this book.

older advisors and priests. Under their influence and that of his mother Jedidah, the young king took after his great grandfather Hezekiah, for it is said of him that "he did that which was right in the sight of the Lord, and walked in all the way of David his father, and turned not aside to the right hand or to the left" (22:2).

This was a time of transition in the Near East. For many years the might of the Assyrian empire had cast a long shadow across that part of the world. But now that power was beginning to crumble. And crumble it did some twenty-five years after Josiah became king of Judah. The rival of Assyria, Babylon, had formed a coalition with the Medes and Scythians, and in 612 B.C. Assyria was conquered. Babylon was now a powerful force in the Near East, opening the way for the fulfillment of Isaiah's prediction in Hezekiah's day (20:14–18).

Excavations of the pagan temple at Arad in southern Judah. The altar and associated pillars are visible. This temple is thought to have been destroyed by King Josiah in his reformation of 621 B.C.

A Dramatic Discovery

When young King Josiah's period of training was over and he was around twenty-six years old, he gave detailed instructions to renovate the Jerusalem Temple. This was begun under the direction of a scribe named Shaphan and Hilkiah the high priest (22:3–7).

As the old Temple was being repaired, an exciting discovery was made. Probably in the dark recesses of some abandoned room in the Temple a book—scroll—was found and identified as "the book of the law" (22:8). Some early scholars identified this book as the Pentateuch; however, the majority opinion leans to the idea that it was a long-lost copy of the Book of Deuteronomy. But the important thing is that when the contents of the book were read, Josiah and all who heard it realized the full extent of the disobedience that had prevailed in Judah. After all, the Book of Deuteronomy spells out in no uncertain terms the disciplines involved in being faithful to God and the penalties for being unfaithful.

Early in Deuteronomy there is a restatement of the commandments given to Moses on Mount Sinai (Deut. 5:6–21). Immediately following that we have what has come to be known as the *Shema* (Deut. 6:4–15), which begins, "Hear, O Israel: the Lord our God is one Lord: And thou shalt love the Lord thy God with all thine heart, and with all thy soul, and with all thy might" And to love God that way illuminates the ancient word, "Thou shalt love thy neighbour as thyself" (Lev. 19:18).

Loving God according to the Book of Deuteronomy calls for a sensitivity to the needs of the poor (Deut. 15:1–18; 23:19–20; 24:14–15, 19–22). Loving God also means care for our neighbor (Deut. 22:8). The Book of Deuteronomy speaks of the need to build a society that reflects the justice, love, and mercy of the God who brought Israel out of slavery in Egypt (Deut. 5:15; 15:15; 16:12; 24:18–20). This was radically different from the way the people of Judah had understood their social and spiritual responsibilities.

As the impact of the words from this lost scroll

began to strike King Josiah, we're told that "he rent his clothes"—he tore his clothes—as a sign of repentance. Then he instructed the spiritual leaders of Judah to "enquire of the Lord for me, and for the people, and for all Judah, concerning the words of this book" (22:11–13). In these words was a command: Hilkiah, Ahikam, Achbor, and Shaphan were to find someone who could clearly interpret what all of this meant.

The reading of this Word of the Lord inspired Josiah to action, as it has done for sincere, repentant, and obedient people of every century since. The writer of the Book of Hebrews spoke of the impact of God's Word in colorful and descriptive language, "For the word of God is quick, and powerful, and sharper than any twoedged sword, piercing even to the dividing asunder of soul and spirit, and of the joints and marrow, and is a discerner of the thoughts and intents of the heart" (Heb. 4:12).

As we read and study the Bible, it becomes a life-changing power in our lives. In speaking of God's Word, General Ulysses S. Grant said, "The Bible is the sheet anchor of our liberties. Write its principles upon your heart and practice them in your lives." General Grant's counterpart in the army of the Confederacy, Robert E. Lee, once said, "The Bible is a book in comparison with which all others in my eyes are of minor importance, and which in all my perplexities and distresses has never failed to give me light and strength." And somewhere, Dr. A. W. Tozer, gifted preacher and writer, expressed clearly the penetrating power of God's Word, "I did not go through the Book. The Book went through me." This is what happened to Josiah as he heard the words in the scroll read aloud, and it is what will happen to us, even in the daily routines of our lives, as under the guidance of the Holy Spirit we hear and act on the Word of God.

Huldah, the Prophetess

The story takes a unique twist now. The delegation commissioned by Josiah to consult with someone who could interpret the meaning of the scroll went to see a woman who lived in the "college" or "second quarter" of Jerusalem (22:14–20). Little is known of the prophetess Huldah, except that her husband's father was the "keeper of the wardrobe"—the one in charge of the priests' vestments. It isn't clear as to why the delegation consulted with Huldah when in all probability Jeremiah, Nahum, and Zephaniah were active as God's spokesmen in Judah at this time.

Speaking fearlessly, Huldah prefaced her words to the delegation by citing the authority for what she was about to say: "Thus saith the Lord . . ." Then she went on to make clear that since the people of Judah have not followed the principles of the Law as it had been given to Moses, they must pay the consequences of their disobedience and sin. Because of their idolatry over the years the price they were to pay was rejection by the Lord. At the same time, she reassured King Josiah that because of his faithfulness he would be spared from being a part of that final tragedy because it would not occur until after his death (22:18–20).

King Josiah's Crusade

With the full meaning and implications of the scroll clearly defined, King Josiah initiated a great reform movement (23:1–25). First he called a convocation of all the people of Jerusalem and Judah and had the contents of the newly found book read to them. Next the king committed himself to follow and obey the provisions of the book, and his declaration was followed by the commitment of all the people to be obedient to the Law of God (23:1–3).

Then began the massive destruction of the idols, the pagan altars, and the "high places" throughout Judah (23:4–14). The pagan priests were displaced and all forms of Canaanite worship were destroyed. There was a massive housecleaning as anything and everything associated with pagan worship was obliterated.

Next we're told that Josiah's reform extended to the idols and the shrine at Bethel in the former northern kingdom of Israel, where he destroyed the molten bull-calves of Jeroboam's as well as the pagan "high place" shrines in Samaria (23:15–20). Not only were all forms of Canaanite worship wiped out in Samaria, but the pagan priests were killed. Josiah's purge of all forms of pagan worship was complete both in Samaria and in Judah. With the purge completed, King Josiah returned to Jerusalem where, for the first time in three-quarters of a century, the Passover Feast was observed according to the Law as prescribed in Deuteronomy 16:1–8.

Then, as a final step in King Josiah's spiritual reforms, we are told that he abolished all forms of fortune telling and witchcraft and all small household gods or images. So complete was Josiah's reform movement that the Kings writer says of him, "And like unto him [Josiah] was there no king before him, that turned to the Lord with all his heart, and with all his soul, and with all his might, according to all the law of Moses; neither after him arose there any like him" (23:25). King Josiah's reforms gave him a place of greatness along with Hezekiah among all the kings of Judah, yet they came too late to save the southern kingdom of Judah from the coming destruction—the consequence of their sins of idolatry and disobedience for so many years (23:26–27).

Josiah's Death

With startling brevity we are told of Josiah's death (23:28–30). Before Egyptian Pharaoh Necho II was enthroned, Nineveh and Assyria were overrun by the Babylonian coalition in 612 B.C. Because of the treaty between the Assyrians and Egyptians, it is likely Necho and his army were going north to the aid of what was left of the Assyrian forces. King Josiah somehow became involved in a clash with Necho's forces at Megiddo and was killed on the field of battle. Our Kings writer then says that Josiah was taken back to Jerusalem and buried. However, in the parallel account the writer of Chronicles elaborates a bit more: "And all Judah and Jerusalem mourned for Josiah. And Jeremiah lamented for Josiah: and all the singing men and the singing women spake of Josiah in their lamentations to this day" (2 Chron. 35:24–25).

Four Hopeless and Helpless Kings

After Josiah's sudden death his third son Jehoahaz succeeded him to the throne of Judah by popular acclaim (23:30–34). Yet his brief biography indicates he reigned as king for only three months, and in spite of his early promise "he did that which was evil in the sight of the Lord." While we're given no details it is clear that Egypt cast long shadows of difficult days across Judah—Jehoahaz was deposed by Pharaoh Necho and thrown into prison, where he died.

Josiah's second son Eliakim, renamed Jehoiakim, succeeded his brother as king (23:34–24:7). An evil and foolish man, he was nothing more than a puppet of the king of Egypt. His eleven-year reign in Jerusalem from 608 to 598 B.C. marked an infamous time in Judah's history. It was during this time that Nebuchadnezzar arose to power in Babylon and then soundly defeated Pharaoh Necho II, after which he proceeded to overrun Jerusalem. At first Jehoiakim was imprisoned but was then released to be a vassal king under Babylon's dominance. The prophet Jeremiah spoke out against the evil of those days (Jer. 22, 26, 36), but was unable to curb the direction of the people.

After Jehoiakim's death two more kings appeared on the scene in short order. Jehoiachin, Jehoiakim's son, was a teenager and ruled for only three months (24:8–16). It was during this time that Nebuchadnezzar once again laid siege to Jerusalem. The Babylonian threat was ever present. Little Judah was no match for their might, and the first wave of Jews, including Jehoiachin, were taken captive and transported to Babylon.

The last king of Judah, Zedekiah, Jehoiachin's uncle, succeeded his nephew at the whim of Nebuchadnezzar (24:18–20). He reigned as a weakling king for eleven years, from 598 to 587 B.C. We're told that "he did that which was evil in the sight of the Lord," and finally that he staged a rebellion against Nebuchadnezzar.

The Capture and Destruction of Jerusalem

As the Kings writer moves toward the end of his story, we have his colorful picture of the tragic Babylonian siege of Jerusalem. These were painfully dark days as the Babylonian army surrounded and eventually leveled the city (25:1–21). King Zedekiah and his family were captured, and Zedekiah's sons were killed before his eyes. Then he was blinded and taken as a captive to Babylon, where he died (Ezek. 12:13).

A few months after the capture of Jerusalem, Nebuchadezzar sent "Nebuzaradan, captain of the guard" to Jerusalem with instructions to completely demolish the city (25:8). It was then that the Temple was leveled, along with the walls and the buildings of the city. The judgment of God on the southern kingdom of Judah for their sin was complete, as most of the people, especially their leaders, were deported in exile to Babylon.

In the final verses of our Scripture lesson our writer pulls together the loose ends (25:22–30). A man named Gedaliah was appointed governor over Judah by Nebuchadezzar. He made an effort to maintain law and order, but in less than a year he was killed by a group of rebels who then escaped to Egypt.

Twenty-six years after the fall of Jerusalem King Nebuchadnezzar died (550 B.C.?) and was succeeded by Evil-Merodach who, we're told, released King Jehoiachin from prison and allowed him to live out his years in comfort. With this word, the Kings writer closes out his story with a note of hope (25:27–30).

The Prophets

Tracking the final years of the southern kingdom of Judah may at times seem almost irrelevant to us in our late twentieth-century setting. The names of the cast of characters are not only strange but for us nearly unpronounceable. Yet throughout these years we see a God of mercy and grace at work in the hearts of people. Yes, at times they seemed determined to ignore Him and run after the false gods of their day. Then we also see a God who because of their disobedience had them pay the consequences of their sin.

There is much about this bit of history that is depressing, but through it all there were those spiritual ancestors of ours—the prophets—who were faithful in keeping the Word of God before the people. These heroes of the faith model for us God's call in our own lives.

Jeremiah

Jeremiah was a fearless spokesman for God whose preaching ministry in Judah began around 626 B.C. and lasted through the fall of Jerusalem in 587 B.C. We know he was from the small village of Anathoth, located just north of Jerusalem, and that he was from a priestly family and may have served for a time as a priest himself.

Jeremiah was active during King Josiah's reforms. But it was during the reign of Jehoiakim and after the Babylonian victory over the Assyrians that Jeremiah seemed convinced that the southern kingdom of Judah was headed toward disaster. However, as the Book of Jeremiah indicates, the prophet remained faithful to God and to his people through the high moments as well as the low moments.

Jeremiah continued on in Judah after the fall of the city and worked with Governor Gedaliah in an effort to maintain peace under Babylonian rule. The group that murdered Gedaliah took Jeremiah with them when they fled to Egypt, and it was there he died.

While there was much of gloom and foreboding in Jeremiah's ministry, there is throughout all of his preaching the thread of hope as he looked into the future. It has been said of him that he was one of the most Christlike of the prophets.

Nahum

The prophet-poet Nahum came to the forefront sometime during the reign of King Josiah. He credited the Lord with the downfall of the oppressive Assyrian empire (Nineveh) and looked hopefully toward better days for Judah as a result. As a participant in the Josiah revival, he looked ahead with hope to God's deliverance of his people. Nahum wrote with the heart of a poet. His use of vivid description and imagination is unparalleled in prophetic writing.

Zephaniah

Zephaniah was another young poet-prophet during a part of Josiah's reign (1:1). As a city dweller he preached against the corruption and sin of city life. Early in his prophecy he speaks of the Lord sweeping the earth clean (1:2). No less a biblical authority than George Adam Smith in speaking of the Book of Zephaniah wrote, "There is no hotter book in all the Old Testament."

Habakkuk

While we can't be absolutely certain of just when Habakkuk was preaching in Judah, he seems to have been active during that period between 612 and 597 B.C. In all probability he witnessed the Josiah reforms and the rise of the Babylonian empire. From the prophet's writing we also see that he witnessed Judah's darkest days during its death struggle as a nation. Yet through this perceptive man of God we see his hope at work as he gives us the electric words, "The just shall live by his faith" (Hab. 2:4).

The Apostle Paul picked up on this theme when he quoted Habakkuk in Romans 1:17 and Galatians 3:11. The statement, "The just shall live by faith" became Martin Luther's slogan for the Protestant Reformation.

And it was Habakkuk who, in spite of the threats that rocked the kingdom of Judah, could say with confidence, "The Lord is in his holy temple: let all the earth keep silence before him" (Hab. 2:20).

A Closing Word

We have moved in our studies in the Books of Kings from David's declining years to the golden years of Solomon's reign over the united kingdom of Israel. We have traced the movement of God through the years of the divided kingdoms of Israel and Judah to the fall of Israel and the capture of Samaria by the Assyrian army. Then we have progressed steadily through the events of the southern kingdom of Judah until its capture and fall at the hands of the invading Babylonian army under King Nebachadnezzar.

We have seen the Hebrew people and their rulers during those times when they were faithful to the God who had delivered them from Egyptian slavery and had seen them through their years of desert wandering, and into their Land of Promise. But the pages of their history were too often stained by their sins of idolatry and rejection of God.

Through all of this, though, we gain insight into our own Christian pilgrimage as we have seen the faithfulness of God and His incomparable mercy and patience. We learn also not to be discouraged with the seeming hopelessness of events both in our own lives and in world affairs. God is indeed a God of history, and in every period He has His prophets— the people of God—who are faithful to His Word and who constantly point the way to a life of faith. Our challenge is to be that kind of a prophet in our own worlds, in our own neighborhoods and towns!

Lord, You are faithful—even when I am not; You are incompa-rably merciful—yet Your mercy is never exhausted, it never runs out. Thank You for showing me a portion of Your glory. AMEN.

WHAT THIS SCRIPTURE MEANS TO ME
2 Kings 18—25

When I saw the Pool of Siloam in Jerusalem several years ago, I remembered the first time I'd read about it as a child. Richard Halliburton's *Book of Marvels* told about how the young adventurer had found an opening and explored part of the ancient conduit through the rock between the Spring of Gihon and the Pool of Siloam. It had never occurred to me how difficult it would be to bring water into a walled city under siege on a hill. (I guess I'd not noticed that springs were usually in valleys, and fortresses were on hills!) It is amazing to me that the Hezekiah's tunnel we read about in 2 Kings 20 can still be seen in the twentieth century.

Water is so important to our existence. We can survive without food far longer than we can without water. How wonderful that Jesus referred to Himself as "living water."

In 2 Kings 20:21 we read, "And Hezekiah slept with his fathers, and Manasseh his son reigned in his stead." We are told that Hezekiah "did that which was right in the sight of the Lord," and Manasseh "did that which was evil in the sight of the Lord."

The story of the reigns of Hezekiah and Manasseh reminds me of a statement I once heard that we are always "just one generation removed from paganism." Whenever we fail to teach our children about the importance of God in our lives and in their lives—then this is a very real possibility. I wonder why Manasseh didn't follow in his father's footsteps, especially since Hezekiah was a good role model. Perhaps it had to do with his mother Hephzibah's influence on him, for many of the kings married into foreign royal families to enhance their countries' alliances, and these women usually imported their own pagan religions. Or perhaps it was the influence of his peer group or his royal advisors, for he was only twelve years old when he became king. Or it could have been that this was a son in rebellion against his father's ideals. Whatever the cause, Manasseh's choices had disastrous results for Judah. It is interesting, though, that two generations later in the same family Josiah becomes a king who "did that which was right in the sight of the Lord" (22:2).

I recall being fascinated with Sunday school stories about Josiah when I was a child. He was referred to as the "boy king," being only eight years old when he came to the throne. The story I liked best was the one about Josiah's standing before all the people and reading God's covenant aloud after it had been found in the Temple. It always seemed strange to me that the Scriptures could be "lost" in the Temple, of all places! I wondered how that could happen. But when I think of things I've "lost" in our attic or garage, it's easier to imagine. When we moved one time I "found" the Bible I had carried in our wedding and the first Bible my mother had given me when I was three years old. They had been packed away through three moves.

But being misplaced is not the only way God's Word can be "lost." It is lost just as much when we don't read it and study it and apply its teachings to our lives. It can be lost when we let schedules crowd it out of our lives. It can be lost when we don't share it with others.

LESSON 8
1 & 2 Chronicles
Another Version

Lord, Use Your Word to change me, teach me, free me. AMEN.

In our study so far we have moved through forty-seven chapters of the Books of 1 and 2 Kings. This has taken us through a period of approximately four hundred years, ranging from the beginning of King Solomon's reign over Israel to the fall of Jerusalem and the release of King Jehoiachin from prison in Babylon (c. 961 to 561 B.C.).

Except for Solomon's golden years these were, for the most part, turbulent times—times of ruthless struggle, political intrigue, vicious warfare—times of unfaithfulness to the God of the Exodus and times of a degrading disregard for spiritual and moral decency. We've seen the people of Israel again and again abandon their noble heritage in favor of the basest forms of pagan worship, including child sacrifice and sexual perversion.

Woven into the story, we've also been shown select men and women of God who have faithfully kept the Word of the Lord before the minds and hearts of the people. At times they were heard and their message was heeded, but all too often the ways of leaders and people "who did that which was evil in the sight of the Lord" prevailed.

Before we plunge into this final lesson of our study, now involving the Books of 1 and 2 Chronicles, let's reflect for a time on what we find in the Bible as a whole. In the early pages of our Bible we have a picture of paradise—of a garden. But then we see Adam and Eve forced from that garden because of their disobedience. A little further on we read about the ups and downs of Abraham and Sarah, of Isaac, Jacob, and Joseph, of the Hebrews living and working as slaves in the hot sun of Egypt. Through the struggle and human misery, we also see God at work doing at times what seems to be the strangest things in the strangest ways as He seeks to mold an obedient people while still leaving with them the power of choice.

Our Bible story is painted in rich and vivid colors as we move with the Hebrews through their wilderness travels and then across the Jordan River into their Land of Promise. And from Joshua through King David's reign the pace is restless and turbulent—a combination of the best of times and the worst of times.

The Land and the People

Most of the action in this ongoing saga of God and His people takes place at the eastern end of the Mediterranean Sea on the land bridge between three continents—an area we know today as Israel, Lebanon and part of Syria. It was crisscrossed in ancient times by strategic trade routes that fed the economies of the Near East. Because of its importance, every surrounding world power and government attempted to occupy and control it. But none held it for long. There was always another power waiting in the wings.

As nations rose and fell through the centuries, many cultures disappeared when their people were absorbed by their conquerors. Only the Hebrews survived both as a people—the Jews—and as a culture—Judaism with its tradition and Scriptures. How and why did this happen?

Between Two Worlds

It happened because the people of Israel had caught a vision that they lived between two worlds. They, as we, saw that this is an imperfect world. People may be good or bad, kind or cruel, but no one is perfectly good. Nor does life work out just as we think it should. Like the ancient Hebrews, we feel in our bones that there must be a better way. Now and then in our moments with God we catch flashes of spiritual reality that clue us in to the potential of better times. Living between these two worlds involves a kind of creative tension, and I believe the Books of 1 & 2 Chronicles focus on this tension.

Imagine, if you will, a young boy growing up in one of our tough inner city neighborhoods thinking that the whole world was made up of asphalt, concrete, filthy alleys, and grubby houses. Then one day he walks several miles from his home neighborhood and catches his first glimpse of a wide expanse of sand with the blue ocean stretching out as far as he can see. It's a whole new world that he never knew existed and it changes his entire outlook on life.

I find reading the Bible to be something like that. The Bible gives me glimpses of a world crammed with truth and beauty and wonder, filled with the presence of God. And reading the Bible heightens the tension in me between the world as I find it and the world my ancestors once lost somewhere east of Eden.

What Now?

So, what now? Well, Judaism as a religion of faith didn't catch on in the luxury of Solomon's court—it came to life only during the difficult days in which the Jews lived in exile. And Christianity began at the cross of Jesus. So often in history the greatest people have died in obscurity—their triumphs only became known later. For example, the Earl of Shaftesbury labored passionately to end the exploitation of children in England. But it took seventeen years to get a law through Parliament limiting a child's working day to ten hours. And it took thirty more years to make the law work!

In our Bible drama we saw Moses die alone on a mountain in the Transjordan without setting foot in the Land of Promise he'd been moving toward for so many years. And Jesus, after selfless years of teaching and preaching the Good News and healing people in need, was betrayed, ridiculed, denied, and then crucified. But He never was cynical nor did He lose heart, and even in death He seemed oddly in control. He persisted in believing that the human heart can be moved by love—and on Easter morning He gave the world the final proof. It's the reality of that kind of a world that is confronted in the two Books of Chronicles.

Chronicles and the Hebrew Scriptures

The first section of the Hebrew Bible—Genesis, Exodus, Leviticus, Numbers, and Deuteronomy— became for the Jewish people the most sacred part of their Scriptures and was known as the Torah. Next in importance came the Prophets. This section began with Joshua and ran through 2 Kings, followed by the Books of Isaiah through Malachi. When Jesus spoke of the Law and the Prophets, He was referring to these two sections.

The remaining books in what we refer to as the Old Testament were lumped together in what the Jews called "the Writings." These included such books as Ruth, Job, Psalms, Proverbs, Daniel. The last books in this section and in the Hebrew Bible were what we know as 1 and 2 Chronicles.

It would be quite easy for the uninitiated reader to question the need for the presence of the two Books of Chronicles in our Scriptures. After all, it seems as though we are reading an exact repetition of what we have already read in the Books of Samuel and Kings. To the casual reader, this appears to be a senseless and boring repetition that we wouldn't miss if it wasn't there.

However, the Books of Samuel and Kings were in written form before the fall of Jerusalem in 587 B.C. They offered a history of Israel through all the years of the monarchy and were available to the people in exile in Babylon as reminders of their past and as interpreters of why they found themselves in exile in Babylonia instead of enjoying their land of inheritance. This means that the Books of Samuel and Kings came from writers with the perspective of national life before the rape and destruction of Jerusalem.

A Quick History Lesson in Parentheses

At the end of the Books of Kings we are told that many of the people of Judah were transported east to Babylon as captives. All that they knew and held dear was left behind, including the ruins of their capital city of Jerusalem. We know that this period of forced exile lasted roughly fifty years. And it was during this time that prophets like Ezekiel and Jeremiah helped the Jews to see that their exile was in reality the disciplining hand of God.

Following King Nebuchadnezzar's death, his kingdom began to crumble, and within a few years Babylon was invaded and conquered by the Persian army. The Persians had an altogether different attitude toward the Judean exiles. They were much more humane and ultimately opened the way for the exiles to return home to Judah.

The Beginnings of Judaism

It was during their years in exile, away from the Jerusalem Temple, that Judaism developed, as did synagogue worship. The people of Israel began to see themselves as a worshiping community rather than a national community. Both their history and their religious life came to be viewed through a new set of lenses.

When the Persian King Cyrus gave the Jews permission to return home to Judah and Jerusalem, many of them had become comfortable—and probably even prosperous in their exile—so they remained in Babylon. However, three waves of people did make their way back west to reclaim their land.

The Samaritans

When the returnees got back to Judah and Jerusalem, they discovered that many of the people left behind when the northern kingdom of Israel had been conquered by the Assyrians had intermarried with the Assyrians who had been brought out west to resettle the land. This made them sort of a mongrel race—neither Jew nor Assyrian. In addition, they had set up their own worship center in Samaria and accepted only part of the Torah as their Scripture. This mixed race—part Jew and part Assyrian—became the ancestors of the Samaritans we read about in the New Testament.

The returning exiles with their "true blue" Jewish blood tried to ignore their northern neighbors and wanted nothing to do with them. This only served to alienate the Samaritan folks, who then set about to do everything they could to frustrate and harass the Judeans. All of this is graphically told in the Books of Ezra and Nehemiah.

This background explains the strong feelings in New Testament times between the Samaritans and the Jews. Then, if a good Jew was traveling north from Jerusalem to somewhere in Galilee, he would go miles out of his way to avoid the direct route through Samaria. This is why, when Jesus was traveling through Samaria and asked the woman at the well at Sychar for a drink of water, she asked in so many words, "How come you, a Jew, even speak to me?" And this is why it was such a shock to His listeners when Jesus made the hero of His story about the traveling man who was robbed and beaten on the road to Jericho a Samaritan.

And so the mindset of the Jewish people who had returned from exile in Babylon to start a new order in their homeland was entirely different from what it had been before. No longer did they see themselves as a politically ambitious state with military significance. Instead, they now shaped their lives around the Torah as administered by the priests.

This simply meant that the writer of what we know of as Chronicles, while drawing his information almost entirely from the early documents of Samuel and Kings, was viewing the history of the monarchy period from a different perspective. Incidentally, the Hebrew name for Chronicles is "Words of the Days"—the events of the times. Our title grew out of Jerome's translation of the Hebrew Old Testament into Latin in which he referred to these books as a chronicle of divine history.

The writer of Chronicles, generally referred to as the Chronicler, was now writing for Jews who had returned to their homeland from foreign exile, so that his perspective was to help his readers view their history from a spiritual and religious point of view. This simply meant that he selected material and events which fulfilled this particular purpose. He wanted his readers to understand above everything else who and what they were as the people of God. In other words, he was less concerned with their

Enter . . . the Books of Chronicles

163

national and political roots and was concentrating on their spiritual roots—their heritage as God's chosen people. This doesn't mean that the Chronicler was attempting to rewrite history. Quite the contrary. There is every indication he had profound respect for what had already been written. But he wanted his readers to have the whole story.

In Chronicles we also get a sense of God's grace and inclusiveness. He seems to be speaking out against any thought that only those in Judah—the self-righteous remnant—were the people of God. In reading Chronicles you will see that the writer refers over and over again to "all Israel."

The application of the Chronicler's idea is certainly clear for us in these closing days of the twentieth century. These are not times for divisive nit-picking in the family of God. Rather, in the complexities of a space- and computer-world, people who call upon the name of the Lord need to draw together in unity irrespective of social and cultural differences and nuances of interpretation.

1 Chronicles 1–9

As we move now into this overview of Chronicles, we come to the first main division—the lengthy genealogies that introduce us to all that is to follow. From our point of view this monotonous list of names is meaningless and strange. But the truth is that these were people—people who were born, grew up, married, had families, worked, and then died. They were people who smiled and frowned, who sweat and cried, who sang and danced. They experienced joy as well as grief, doubt as well as faith. In fact, the people in these lists were our spiritual ancestors.

It isn't likely that you will read these chapters in detail, but if you did, you would find that the genealogy is selective and emphasizes the Chronicler's desire to concentrate on religious history. The list given in Chapter 1 of 1 Chronicles covers the period between Adam and Israel-Jacob. The names found in Chapter 2 comprise the descendants of Judah up to the time of David. In Chapter 3 we have David's descendants listed to a post-exilic time, and

Chapter 4 continues the select list of Judah's descendants.

We can readily see that the Chronicler considered the Judah genealogy to be of vital importance, because he devoted the equivalent of three chapters to it. You will note that mention is made of the line of Simeon in Chapter 4:24–43. But by the time of this writing Simeon was no longer a separate tribe, and for the most part had fused with Judah.

Next follows the genealogies of the tribes that settled east of the Jordan (5:1–26). Then, because of his preoccupation with spiritual history, all of Chapter 6 (81 verses) is devoted to the tribe of Levi—the priestly tribe and especially the descendants of Aaron.

In Chapter 7 we have the genealogy of the northern tribes with the exception of Benjamin, and in Chapter 8 we find the genealogy of Benjamin. Most of the Benjamin territory was in the hands of Judah following the return from exile. Finally, Chapter 9 lists the family names of a select group, some of whom were associated with Temple worship.

David Is Introduced by the Chronicler

In just a few words the Chronicler writes off the reign of King Saul (1 Chron. 10:1–14). From his point of view there was little religious significance to that period in Israel's history. To the Jews who had returned from Babylonian exile and were struggling to rebuild Jerusalem and reestablish themselves in the Land of Promise, David's name and example was all important. Consequently, our writer devotes considerable space to a review of David's reign as king of Israel and as the one who looked ahead to the day when the Temple of the Lord would be the heart of Jerusalem (11:1–29:30).

David as a Religious Leader

As we read these chapters in our Scripture lesson devoted to King David, we become aware of the Chronicler's selectivity in creating his history. Compared to the Samuel account our present writer includes only those events which represent David as a spiritual leader. He omits any episodes and events that picture David differently. So the David in the

Chronicles story is not the military and political king under whose leadership Israel achieved greatness in the Near East. Rather, he is the key figure in Israel's pilgrimage from "chosen nation" to "chosen community of faith."

Perhaps in no other place is this more apparent than the marvelous prayer of thanksgiving David prayed toward the end of his reign (1 Chron. 29:10–19). Few words of praise have ever appeared in print that can equal David's prayer. "Blessed be thou, Lord God of Israel our father, for ever and ever. Thine, O Lord, is the greatness, and the power, and the glory, and the victory, and the majesty: for all that is in the heaven and in the earth is thine; thine is the kingdom, O Lord, and thou art exalted as head above all. Both riches and honour come of thee, and thou reignest over all; and in thine hand is power and might; and in thine hand it is to make great, and to give strength unto all. Now therefore, our God, we thank thee, and praise thy glorious name . . . for all things come of thee, and of thine own have we given thee" (29:10–14).

It is significant that this magnificent prayer was given at a great service of worship to dedicate the riches collected for the Temple. Here we see the aged king as a spiritual leader. For the Chronicler it was entirely fitting to drop the curtain on David's life not long after the old king had led his people in a national worship service.

The Importance of Worship

The theme of worship is ever-present in the mind of the Chronicler as he writes. He shows us that David's main concern was the central place of worship in Jerusalem. In 1 Chronicles 13 through 15 we have the story of the moving of the Ark of the Covenant into Jerusalem. The Ark was the symbol of God's presence among His people, and now that it was located in Jerusalem, David saw to it that regular services of worship were once again held.

In reading these three chapters we can't help but be impressed with the detail and care that went into the service of worship. In the hymn of praise that followed the establishment of the Ark in Jerusalem, we recognize excerpts from the Psalms which were

used in worship. We would do well to be reminded
regularly of the closing words of this hymn, "O give
thanks unto the Lord; for he is good; for his mercy
endureth forever. . . . Blessed be the Lord God of
Israel for ever and ever" (1 Chron. 16:34, 36).

As David looked back over his life, he knew that
worship of the Lord was at the very heart of the
Jewish faith. It was a legacy that was supposed to
make a difference in the way people lived and acted.
By contrast a modern critic described worship as a
group of conventional people gathered each week to
be addressed by a conventional little person who
tried to persuade them to be more conventional. The
following conversation illustrates the criticism:

"Are you going to church?"
"Yes."
"What do you do when you go to church?"
"Well, nothing. Oh, sometimes I teach Sunday
school. But when I go into church, I don't do any-
thing. I don't sing in the choir. I'm not an usher. I just
go."
"But when you go, don't you do anything?"
"No, I just sit and listen."
"Just listen?"
"Well, I try to sing the hymns. I put my money in
the offering plate as it goes by, and when the
preacher prays, I close my eyes, if that's what you
mean."
"Do you *worship?*"
"Oh, well, yes, I guess we all do that."

Unfortunately, this casual attitude toward worship is all too prevalent in our churches today. And
it completely misses the true meaning of worship,
which is to focus on the Lord and in so doing be
challenged to do and achieve our best. Some of this
misunderstanding of worship is illustrated by a contrast a colleague of mine, Dr. John Anderson, makes.
Whenever he misses a church service he tends to ask
someone who has been present, "What did the
preacher *say?*" But whenever his teenaged son misses
a service, he is more likely to ask, "What did they
do? What happened?"

It seems to me that Dr. Anderson's teenage son is closer to the truth. True worship inspires us to action, to service. David knew that true worship was not a passive thing. And so, in the closing verses of 1 Chronicles 29, the writer tells us that after David prayed, the people offered sacrifices as prescribed by the Law, and they "did eat and drink before the Lord on that day with great gladness" (29:21–22). There was nothing casual about their worship. They wouldn't have said, "I guess we all do that." Instead we read, "And all the congregation blessed the Lord God of their fathers, and bowed down their heads, and worshipped the Lord."

Why Do People Worship?

As minister to a late-twentieth-century congregation I frequently ask myself on Sunday morning, "Why have they come?" To such a question I can imagine a variety of answers, but I have to believe that central to most of them is the desire to receive a word from the Lord. This desire certainly prompted worship in ancient Israel and was carried forward into the New Testament.

In speaking of Jesus on one occasion Luke wrote, "And he came to Nazareth, where he had been brought up: and, as his custom was, he went into the synagogue on the sabbath day" (Luke 4:16). As the story of Jesus unfolds we see Him gathering twelve disciples around Himself, the small group which became a nucleus of a larger group—the Christian church of the New Testament. Jesus was concerned about worship and the worshiping community.

From the days of the Jewish exiles' return from Babylon to the present, people have come together to worship in a house of God because of a common need for God and for fellow believers. Neither at the time Chronicles was written nor in the time of the New Testament church did anyone doubt that faith was much more than merely an individual's personal relationship to God.

From the time of Chronicles on, the pattern for the people of God has called for us to come together in worship. I don't find any isolated believers in the New Testament. And so my faith in Christ means that I must meet with others who believe. What else do such words as these mean, "Where two or three are gathered together in my name, there am I in the midst of them" (Matt. 18:20)? That's why we come to worship—to know and celebrate that Presence!

As New Testament Christians came together regularly to celebrate the presence of the risen Christ, certain forms of worship began to take shape under the leadership of the Apostle Paul and the other evangelists of the first century. During the following centuries worship patterns within the church have taken different forms and have also had to undergo times of reformation.

Noteworthy among the reformation times was the seventeenth century, when reformers corrected the cold ritualism that had paralyzed the church. Worshipers had become spectators instead of participants. The reality of the presence of Christ "where two or three are gathered together in my name," was lost and had to be recovered. "There am I"—nothing else ultimately matters. Worship, the constant exposure of our lives to the highest we know, to the presence of God, is our salvation. That makes worship a love affair! It is the most thrilling and heartwarming activity there is—a personal encounter of the creature with the Creator, the soul with the Savior. That's not religion; it is *Life!*

One Generation to Another

As the Chronicles writer gets ready to lower the curtain on David's reign as king of Israel, we see Solomon poised to take over. The great longing of David's heart to build a house for the Lord was not to be. But David could rest secure in the fact that Solomon, his son, would build the house (1 Chron. 28:6). The sceptor was now to be passed from father to son. "Thus David the son of Jesse reigned over all Israel. And the time that he reigned over Israel was forty years; seven years reigned he in Hebron, and thirty and three years reigned he in Jerusalem. And he died in a good old age, full of days, riches, and honour" (1 Chron. 29:26–28a).

Solomon, the Son of David

The second Book of Chronicles opens with these words, "And Solomon the son of David was strengthened in his kingdom, and the Lord his God was with him, and magnified him exceedingly" (1:1).

Chapters 1 through 9 of 2 Chronicles give us the

169

story of Solomon as seen through the eyes of the Chronicler. The writer views Solomon's history, as he did David's, more from the religious perspective than the political. Solomon is seen as the builder of the Temple, the fulfillment of David's dream.

The Temple is planned for and it is built. Then comes the marvelous ceremony of dedication followed by the awesome words, "The glory of the Lord filled the house" (2 Chron. 7:1).

Following the dedication ceremonies, the Chronicler tells us that the Lord appeared to Solomon at night and said, "I have heard thy prayer, and have chosen this place to myself for an house of sacrifice. If I shut up heaven that there be no rain, or if I command the locusts to devour the land, or if I send pestilence among my people; *If my people, which are called by my name, shall humble themselves, and pray, and seek my face, and turn from their wicked ways; then will I hear from heaven, and will forgive their sin, and will heal their land"* (2 Chron. 7:12–14, italics mine).

Here we see the Temple as a place of worship and a place where prayer will be answered. Here, too, is the eternal promise that as we turn to God and confess our sins, He will forgive. The writer of John's first letter said it clearly, "If we confess our sins, he is faithful and just to forgive us our sins, and to cleanse us from all unrighteousness" (1 John 1:9).

Before the Lord was through with Solomon that night, He had something more to say. He promised that if Solomon lived a faithful life like his father David had, He would be with him and Solomon would prosper (2 Chron. 7:17–18). On the other hand, if Solomon turned his back on the Lord, he and his descendants would be set aside. While the Chronicler doesn't give us the details, we know from the Kings writer that Solomon fell far short of what the Lord had desired.

Again, through the combined writings of Kings and Chronicles, we see that God works with and through frail human instruments. In the life of Solomon, as in the life of his father David, we see the patience and mercy of God. And we find reassurance in the fact that even as God worked in and through them, He will with us if we let Him.

The achievements, wealth, and wisdom of Solomon were stupendous. But Jesus summarized and then dismissed the glory of Solomon with a single sentence: "Consider the lilies of the field, how they grow; they toil not, neither do they spin: And yet I say unto you, That even Solomon in all his glory was not arrayed like one of these" (Matt. 6:28–29). Jesus lets us know that because no one is more important than anyone else to God, everyone is special. And since "God is no respecter of persons," We are to respect all persons.

The Rest of the Story

The remainder of the Book of 2 Chronicles, Chapters 10 through 36, gives us the lugubrious scenario of Rehoboam and his successors in the southern kingdom of Judah. The Chronicler has very little to say about the northern kingdom of Israel. He tends to emphasize the preservation of Jewish identity and the avoidance of sins against the Law. And we begin to see the rise of Judaism as an exclusive community with a unique religious witness. Further, as we read between the lines we begin to catch a hint of the Chronicler's hope of a coming messianic kingdom with a son of David as its head.

In the meantime, though, the political state of Judah slides rapidly downhill, caught in the power politics of the superpowers of that day. Finally, Nebuchadnezzar's army destroys Jerusalem and the Temple, and carries off everything of value. The kingdom of Judah is no more.

As we read the Books of Kings and Chronicles, we can't help but be amazed at the power of the living God who often does the strangest things in the strangest ways. Yet, somehow, I get the feeling that the story here leaves us standing on the border of a Promised Land. And I also get the feeling that a New David will soon bring in a New Era based on a New Promise to a New People, "For unto you is born this day in the city of David a Saviour, which is Christ the Lord" (Luke 2:11).

Father, You are all powerful, majestic, and glorius. AMEN!

171

WHAT THIS SCRIPTURE MEANS TO ME
1 & 2 Chronicles

Ever since the publication of Alex Haley's *Roots,* people have shown an increased interest in tracing their own "roots." Several people I know have not only done research on their family tree in libraries, but they have also made trips half-way across the country to visit cemeteries and pore over records in county courthouses. The ones I know who have enjoyed it the most have interviewed older members of their family and written histories and anecdotes for their children. Several have coupled this with cassette recordings or videos and compiled photo albums for each child—complete with names, dates, and places. What a wonderful gift for present and future generations!

Several years ago when my husband and I were in California, we enjoyed visiting some of his father's relatives who had moved there during the "dust bowl" days of the Great Depression. We were surprised to learn that the three families who had originally moved had now grown to number about fifty persons. And it was fun to meet "cousins by the dozens"!

The Books of Chronicles contain chapters and chapters of genealogies, and I guess I've frequently been guilty of skipping all the "begats" as too tedious to read. But then I realized that this was a record of how God placed us in families who relate to each other and who influence the lives of those who are yet to be born. Each family has its own list of relatives who are admired—as well as its own "black sheep."

Part of the way I can understand who I am is to learn something about my family's past history. The Chronicler knew this and reminded the people of Israel about the people who came before them. He reminded them of their relationship to their ancestors and of how God had led His people through the great events in their history.

I've filled out the "family tree" pages in our children's baby books so they'll know the names of some of their ancestors. And my father's family has a family Bible in which my grandfather had listed the names and the dates of birth of each of his twelve children.

As much as my own family genealogy means to me, though, I'm aware that I also have a "spiritual genealogy." There are people to whom I'm "related" because of their importance in my Christian life—Mrs. Dees, my childhood Sunday school superintendent; Mr. Walden, an older friend at church; Dr. Leslie Williams, a college Bible professor who gave me a job and friendship and advice when I needed it as a young adult.

These people, and many others, are an important part of my "genealogy," too.

When I become discouraged I like to recall the ways in which God has been with me through the good times and difficult times. And often I do this best in church as I worship. The Chronicler included much about the worship of God and the Temple because this was one of the central experiences that kept Israel together as a people. Church puts me in the mood to "count my blessings." And one of the things for which I am grateful is that God "setteth the solitary in families" (Psa. 68:6).

Index

References to illustrations are given in italics.